Eye

Contact

How to Alter Your Eye Contact

(How It Can Be Used for Manipulation and Control)

Matthew Marshall

Published By **Simon Dough**

Matthew Marshall

Eye Contact: How to Alter Your Eye Contact (How It Can Be Used for Manipulation and Control)

ISBN   978-1-990373-87-9

Legal & Disclaimer

Table Of Contents

Chapter 1: Why is Eye Contact Important?

Based on Adrian Furnham, Ph.D. Professor of Psychology from University College London, the topic of eye contact from the 1960s to the present was viewed as a nebulous unnecessary waste of time. Our culture today, however, cannot attribute greater significance to our gaze even should it try. Eyes are the eyes of our souls. They transmit our emotions and thoughts as well as our essence to the people around us. Eye contact is the oldest, and still until today, the most efficient method of communicating.

Eye contact can create a strong emotional connection between two individuals which reveals often too clearly, the real issues within our minds and hearts. Anger, humiliation, guilt and depressed feelings cause us to turn our backs on people around us, but however we tend to spend more time looking into the eyes with people we cherish and admire and admire. The nature of our relationships on the basis of eye contact. The more eye contact there is an eye contact, the more intimate is the bond. However, according to Goman that the degree of eye contact is also contingent on whether it is voluntarily or forceful. In particular, individuals tend to stay clear of eye contact when they are in bus stations, elevators that are crowded as well as other scenarios where they are near physical proximity with strangers.

The boundary between insufficient and excessive eye contact can be a blur. When it comes to personal interactions excessive eye contact can be intimidating, hostile or rude. If it's a workplace setting the message could be seen as a strategy to dominate the other, to intimidate, or lower the standing of another in order to gain the advantage. The effects of all these regardless of whether they are intentional or not, cause defense on the part of the individual or persons who have your gaze. And for many people, the necessity to defend yourself doesn't provide any room for connection as well as trust, or even a need to connect with you to come back in the near future.

However, excessive eye contact may damage relationships, albeit for different motives. Both in business and personal situations, it could cause you to appear uneasy and, if that happens people around you or others present might think about what's incorrectly, making the other person feel uneasy as well. This also creates an impression of looking around for the answers that make you appear in a state of confusion. In western society, we put an emphasis on the way we look in judging an individual's honesty. One could interpret the inability of you to look them in the eye as an indication you're lying, or you aren't interested in their opinions or anything they've got to tell you.

Of course, the optimal level of eye contact differ from one circumstance to the next. As an example, speaking in a meeting for business is not going to require the same quantity or type of eye contact. Neither will the flirting process with someone you'd like to get acquainted with. You will not make the identical degree of eye contact conversation with the eyes of a Muslim woman like you would in a conversation with an atheist male who is from New York City. It is interesting to note that eye contact differs between males and females. Women are more likely to enjoy face-to-face discussions, whereas men feel more comfortable speaking in a row.

When we return to the Goman 2013 Forbes report, I discover that thankfully, there's a simple guideline you can use to apply it to a variety of circumstances. To increase efficiency by creating a relaxed setting, we must utilize direct eye contact for 30 to 60 per cent often. It should also be avoided when speaking and more during watching. Indeed, Furnham tells us, in his article of 2014 entitled "The Secrets of Eye Contact, Revealed," that individuals tend to look for feedback, and also invite other people to talk by looking upwards at the end of a grammatical error or at the end of speaking, thereby using eye contact as a sync signal to give the conversation the feel of a relaxed pace. It is also possible to maintain the flow by looking away when we want to take a moment to think about, reflect, or soften awkward language.

A clear understanding of the best time and length to stare at someone can help you convince and influence them. If used correctly, eye contact can create the impression of trust and the feeling of mutual trust between two people or groups through establishing a sense of trust that everyone feels confident. The majority of highly accomplished people are able to attribute their achievements in part to the assistance of others in some way as it is their trust and respect that inspire people to trust and encourage the realization of their goals. Every salesperson and politician is aware that by making an eye contact with a potential customers or voters to make them appear more credible and genuine. Eye contact is crucial since it's crucial for your success in all area of your life.

The way you employ your gaze is especially important when it comes to beginning new relationships--especially romantic ones. The purpose of looking at someone can be a way to encourage interaction and the more direct your gaze, the more evident the expression of your admiration towards the person you are interested in. The person you are looking at could either acknowledge or decline the invitation simply by turning away or returning their gaze. If intimacy isn't your intention, then you'll need to alter your attitude. When your conversation is more important than the connection between you with the person you're talking to, brief, sporadic gazes can be more productive as opposed to longer-lasting stares. We can also identify the types of relationships that we establish and keep with other people by making the eye in a deliberate specific way.

The length of the gaze isn't its most important characteristic. According to

Furnham it is true that even insignificant factors like the direction eyes, size of eyes, the dilation in pupils and blink speed all transmit massive quantities of information. According to his article from 2014 in Psychology Today article, Furnham discusses a study which demonstrates the effectiveness of only one of the qualities mentioned above--the pupils that are dilation. Participants were shown two photos of women and were they were asked to select which one was the prettiest. In one image the girl's eyes were artificially increased to two times the size they normally have. In other words, the pictures were the exact same. A majority of people were able to see the picture with pupils that were dilate more appealing, but the interesting thing is that most were unable to pinpoint why. Sexual attraction and strong emotions causes pupils to dilate and, without realizing it the human brains take note of this and then reciprocate the effect.

The variety of scenarios where human beings have to create, alter, or alter eye contact to influence others or enhance likability, is virtually limitless. Furnham mentions that Catholic confessory and couches for psychiatric patients are set up in order to limit eye contact as well as the degree of embarrassment and humiliation that the priest suffers. The hitchhiker, as well as people who hitchhike and Salvation Army Santa ringing his bell in front of the mall also make eye contact more frequent in order to draw attention and convince other people to help their goals. Eye contact is also a way to communicate your desire to collaborate or to compete.

An understanding of how to make eye contact can ensure that individuals, regardless of their age, gender or background regardless of the circumstance

9

are able to feel at ease around your persona, feel confident around you and maybe even love them. What you do with your eyes usually has more impact than what you speak to them.

Chapter 2: Why is Eye Contact so Uncomfortable?

Contact with the eyes is one of our most effective and oldest method for communication. It is vital to our survival and our progress in life...but this doesn't mean it's anything less uncomfortable. The reason that eye contact can be not pleasant is because it increases self-awareness dramatically and, consequently can lead to a rise in self-consciousness. It is also more emotional stimulated when they look at them straight on as opposed to look away.

For people who have issues with self-esteem The combination of increased emotionality and increased self-awareness could cause pain. It is natural to wonder what the person is sharing our eyes with is seeing us in the same way that we think of ourselves. Does he see my huge zit and wondering what type of disease I'm suffering from? Do she see my loved-handles? Do you think he believes I'm overweight?

When we come into the first eye contact with a person the inner critic goes into full speed. The same time our eyes become more observant of the faces of others which can lead us to imagine looks that are a sign of condescension, disgust or arrogance but aren't. At the same time, we are able to project our negativity about ourselves on the person we're talking to. As a result of the increased emotional intensity and heightened emotional state, we are more prone to react at the judgements we imagine that the person we are talking to is saying about us.

Eye contact can also create an extremely strong bond between two individuals. If someone is looking straight into your eyes at first, you might feel that your relationship took an abrupt shift from being informal to intimate. If you're unprepared to be intimate with the person or are not looking to get close to the person, the sudden change can be very uncomfortable. It's as if the internal workings of each individual's soul and mind were displayed to the entire public who are watching in excitement as trying to communicate in a way that creates a sense of common space in which it is possible to live comfortably. It's like being on stage and being able to see the thoughts of every members as they formulate views about you.

A feeling of discomfort or discomfort are more intense in people who are introverts or very empathetic in their nature. Certain types of personalities are so sensitive and alert that they don't have to stare at someone at the eye to sense their mood and emotions. If they are, the ferocity of their signals may make them feel that they're being snatched away or trapped in mind and thoughts of another.

In addition, excessive eye contact may be seen as threatening and can be unaffordable for sufferers of the disorder of social anxiety (SAD). An increased than normal fear response can be a sign of SAD which is triggered through a long or direct look from a stranger. Eye contact is especially difficult for people who suffer from autism. Understanding all the diverse aspects of someone else's eye is quite a challenge. It is necessary to interpret lights reflections as well as pupil dilation bleeding capillaries as well as eye movements, in addition to the duration and intensity of eye. While doing this we need to pay attention the spoken word and try to apply nuanced, subtle social and cultural norms so that we can formulate the correct reaction. To do all this simultaneously requires us to be multitasking, which can be exceptionally difficult for people who have autism. Because of this, the impact of eye contact may be too much to handle, leading to sensory oversaturation.

We live our daily life without understanding the nature of eye contact yet we feel uncomfortable and awkward. Understanding the workings behind the procedure may at first cause it to appear more complicated and confusing, however cutting it down into different components allows us to look at each element more carefully and discover how of them are linked. Understanding how eye contact functions lets us use the process to our advantage. There are a variety of effective ways for making eye contact more pleasant as well as being utilized in everyday contexts, workplace situations or when engaging in social activities.

It's difficult to acknowledge our mistakes, however by admitting that you need to focus on the art of eye contact you've made the first step towards developing your social and conversational abilities. However shy or self-conscious you may be it is possible to master the art of eyes to create successful, healthy connections with other people.

Chapter 3: How to Make Eye Contact Easier

If you feel that eye contact is overwhelming to us, frightening, or too stimulating Engaging in it can only create more anxiety to us as well as those we're interacting with. It's not necessary to be an expert in a matter of hours. A gradual improvement in eye contact can help you build your comprehension and allow for better use. When you've made the effort to learn how to utilize eye contact, will notice that looking at your partner will distract you from the tenseness of your own life as well as your inner self-conscious monologue instead of increasing them.

It's crucial to mention that, if taking this course then you're well conscious of the significance to eye contact as well as the possibility of not utilize the full potential of it. Awareness is the initial and foremost step to learning and becoming more proficient at making eye contact. In addition, this awareness suggests that you could make much more contact with your eyes than you do, however it is causing the effort feel insufficient. In essence, you might be more adept in creating eye contact than you believe you are which is an excellent beginning point.

It will also assist you in keeping your mind in the present that while eye contact plays a significant aspect in the social life of us the modern world is now beginning to develop a deeper appreciation and understanding of various personality types. The majority of people are familiar with the fundamental terms like introvert and extrovert such as. Research into the subject of the causes of autism and social anxiety have led to an increased awareness of how social demands and skills can vary depending on the individual.

That means, regardless of whether you're shy with someone, your conversation partner can allow you to express your personality instead of accusing you of being weirdo.

Making more eye contact can be as trying to make improvements in the quality of your food. If you decide to cut down on all the cheeseburgers, sweets, and pizza in one go and stock your fridge with fresh vegetables. There's a chance that you can keep this up for around a week then you'll be tempted to indulge and fall back into routine. The experts advise that the most effective way to change your the way you eat is to slowly include healthy meals into your menu and let these to substitute for unhealthy one by one over the course of the course of. This is the same for eyes. It's not necessary to head to the most popular bar to stare relentlessly at the person who you first meet. In fact you can enhance your eye contact abilities even without any social interaction.

Research has shown that watching a photo of a person looking directly at the camera triggers the same reactions as making eyes-to-face interaction with the person. To begin you should stay in your home and perform the Google image search to find people. When you see photographs of individuals making eye contact, you should spend a little moments looking at them. When you are confident in this method then apply the same approach for television. You can watch the news and practice to look into the eyes of the anchor while she reads the headlines of the night. News anchors tend to be neutral and largely unassuming So keeping eye contact on the screen won't cause excessively emotional responses. When you're at ease with your news anchor you can move to talk programs. The guests on talk shows are more likely to employ intense facial expressions and express emotions. In looking at each other in the eyes and you'll be able to shift your focus from one person to the next.

As well as making eye contact practice, you should also work on the correct posture. If you're not making eye contact we're usually lost in our personal thoughts. Our eyes don't focus and the gaze of our eyes is directed down, which can cause our posture to drop. Standing straight helps you feel more attentive and alert. Your eyes are brought to a point and helps you physically concentrate your eyes on whom you're speaking to. An ideal posture can give your companion the impression that you're curious about the conversation they're having. If you're new to being in a position that is alert and focused It can be exhausting initially, which is why it's best to stand in a straight position while looking at anchors on news programs as well as talk show host.

If you're engaging in eye contact with actual individuals in real-life situations You can gradually work until you can achieve a straight gaze instead of committing to the whole thing immediately. Begin by looking directly at their eyes from behind or between the eyebrows. Most likely, they won't notice any difference. Also, it's not essential to keep eye contact during your entire discussion. Researchers agree that avoiding eye contact when you're talking and more so when you're observing can create the perfect balance to ensure an enjoyable environment. To begin try to make eye contact only while watching the person you are listening to speaking.

Eye contact can also be more effective when it is used for a short time. Once you begin practicing in person, start by engaging in conversations that you are sure won't last for long. As an example, if you drive through and you see the cashier, make sure to look him in the eye as he hand the food. Also, the next time you are at the grocery shop, stare the cashier's eyes when she gives you a receipt. Conversations with cashiers are much easier as they're informal. Conversations with your supermarket cashier can be quite infrequent and therefore, they are less important and therefore there's no pressure to present a flawless impression.

Another way to avoid the eye is to begin making eye contact with your people you know and love. It's less daunting to gaze someone into the eyes when you are familiar with people you know. If you can master making eye contact with those who you are familiar with, you'll be able to transition to those who look like your gorgeous colleague or boss.

If you're one of them, the time to plan your the practice of eye contact will prove immensely beneficial. However, other people could cause stress and confusion. If you find that planning is helpful then go for it. If not, take a shot at making the most eye contact you can when in social settings. The process of planning the practice at home can be beneficial in any case. Making a plan for your home practice can add credibility and significance to your work. This will also make your accountable and force your to work harder that is, as we've all seen will result in more results.

Chapter 4: The Relationship between Eye Contact & Attraction

The findings of researchers have revealed that women in cultures like Papua New Guinea and the United States use the same flirting technique based on eye contact, which has the woman hold his gaze for an extended period of time, before tilting her head downwards and turns away, while smiling. Since this method is common across all cultures and, German ethologist Irenaus Eibl-Eibesfeldt believed that the behaviour was inherent. That means eye contact, as well as being one of the most efficient method of communicating and survival, is our most ancient and effective method of establishing romantic relationships.

In Western cultures, women and men show attraction towards each other by looking at the loved one for about two or three seconds, before lowering their eyes and turning away. Helen E. Fisher tells her readers of her findings in the 1993 Psychology Today article, "The Biology of Attraction," that contact with the eyes triggers an initial part of the brain that responds to either of the two suggested actions: retreat or approach. So when we notice that someone else has fixed their eyes on us and we are unable to resist responding. As we decide whether we want to remain and engage or turn down the invite and run away, we make moves of displacement to ease anxiety about being placed in a position of being put. They're just strategies to delay the decision, such as adjusting the length of your hair or clothes, or looking through your purse or wallet to find something you don't want.

Eye contact triggers instant responses and one of them is dilation of pupils, indication of intense fascination. If your person of interest decides to remain and chat make sure you pay close at their pupils during the discussion. According to the Psychologist Eckhard Hess the pupils dilate in order to let in more light while gazing at someone or a something that we are interested in while they shrink when we focus our attention on things that are less interesting. The concept is applicable to conversations because, whenever we're engaged by the subject at hand our pupils dilate as we become bored of it the pupils contract. If you've caught someone's eye it is crucial to have a good conversation in keeping it. Attention to the activity of your pupils allows you to alter the subject of your discussion so that you can keep them engaged and increase attraction.

Be careful not to study your partner's pupils, though. The constant eye contact can be perceived as an act of aggression or attempt to take over and will certainly make your partner feel uneasy and vulnerable. It can cause feelings of self-consciousness, and can cause another person to turn off and rescind your flirtations.

If you've recently met the individual or person that you're chatting with Try making eye contact for about 50% of the times. Be sure to look at them while they're talking. It gives the impression you're interested in the things they are saying. But, on the other hand it's best to keep your eyes off when discussing. It allows your partner to be able to take in your thoughts without being scolded or put under pressure. They have enough time and space to think about what you're telling them and come up with a suitable response. Studies have also found that people are able to focus when you're not staring into the eyes of someone else, since the intense feelings caused by eye contact could be extremely distracting. Therefore, avoiding looking at your eyes while talking increases the likelihood of saying an intelligent or creative idea.

The direction from which a person is looking while speaking indicates the attraction as well as intention. According psychologists, one is looking to the left when contemplating their past or trying to remember information or experiences. If someone about true tales of their past They are likely to feel at ease in your presence, which can be a signal of affection. Also, the desire to remember facts accurately indicates that someone is trying to impress you by demonstrating their understanding of the subject that is being discussed. In contrast, if a man or woman turns at the right side while speaking and speaking, it is engaging the creative part of their brain. This is, in addition it is used to assist in creating

29

stories. This could mean that the attraction evoked through their non-verbal communication can be a cover to divert your attention from their true intentions. Turning to the left is a common indicator of bored.

The increased frequency of blinks is also an excellent sign of interest as our speed of blinking is likely to grow when we love the person we are with. The wink is another move we make to signal attraction, however even though it's efficient when used correctly however, it could be a bit scary when done incorrectly. In particular, it should not be performed from the side of the bar in a crowd to make your first interaction with a woman that you have never met previously. It is interpreted as sharing secrets, therefore it's possible to interpret as a rather sly gesture. This is more successful and suitable when it is used in conjunction in conjunction with someone you've successfully engaging in a relationship for an hour. Imagine that your friend takes your attention and takes over to see his older brother. The look back at your shoulder and smirking at the girl whom you've been chatting with let her know that you're in love and you'll meet her when you get the chance. When you think about it this way the word "wink" has more of a playful vibe, which can be more appealing than being forward.

In general, eye contact is an accurate sign of romance. Utilize it to make contact when you meet someone, and if the man or lady of your choice chooses to remain and chat you can use eye contact to assess the interest of them and alter the subject of discussion to ensure that they remain interested. Pay attention to them when they speak as well as look away when you're talking. Take note of your pupils and blink rates as well as the direction in which they look as they look away. The above may appear to be an overwhelming amount of information and, in fact, trying to understand all of these messages in a moment, while you're already anxious, can cause confusion and even overwhelm you. Keep in mind that eye contact is the oldest and most reliable method for communications. It is a natural knowledge of how to utilize eye contact. If the idea of eye contact causes you to feel uneasy, practice certain techniques from the previous chapter before attempting to use it when flirting. If not, try to let your mind go and trust your gut instincts. They'll lead you to the right path.

Chapter 5: Tips & Techniques

Even though eye contact is an innate tool for communication and relationship-building, most of us would still like to know how to wield it more effectively. Even those who are the people who are the most daring and confident of people can gain by taking time to improve the way they approach eye contact. In the end, if you're planning to employ one of the most effective tools available to us it's best to make use of it to the fullest capabilities. The techniques listed below can be employed to create and enhance relations of every kind, as well as to increase productivity in every kind of gathering as well as discussions. They can improve every aspect of your parenting skills and your ability to succeed in work.

Before we begin, let's take an in-depth glance at the most successful masters of eye contact, the salesmen political leaders, and motivational speaker who are paid through gaining the respect as well as the trust and respect from others. Everybody including presidential hopefuls to street performers are aware that understanding the importance of eye contact to their achievement. Everyone has walked on the busy streets of downtown at night on a Saturday and witnessed the man standing on the corner, playing his heart out to the beat of his battered guitar. Consider the way you feel when you step up to the open guitar case that is lying on the pavement, half full of loose change and $1 bills. Do you wish to cross the street to keep away from the entertainer or are you tempted to stay watching the performer for an hour and put in the money in your pocket?

You may not have noticed it prior to this, but you select the best course of action for this scenario the same as you decide your plan of action whenever you spot an individual flirting with you. You make your decision based on the way they look at you. If the person on the street engages directly with you and smiles when you come close his stage, the performance will be more personal and enthusiastic as well as you'll probably be more inclined to pay the musician. However If he stares towards the back or to one side, it will make a discord that makes dropping your money into the guitar case seem awkward and uneasy. If you happen to meet a street artist check out his tip-jar, and then into his eyes. If the bin is almost empty, you can be sure the performer won't return your glance.

Eye contact can sell your idea, you and the product you offer, no matter if you're playing your the music in a bustling urban street, or promoting support during a presidential election or asking the CEO of your business to help fund the latest innovative idea. You will have be able to alter your approach to eye contact based on the circumstance and how many people you're speaking to.

In a public speaking situation keep eye contact with the entire audience and not just one individual. If you are focusing solely on one person while you speak your speech, you will lose the attention of your audience. Make sure to shift your attention on a different individual each when you start the next sentence. It keeps everyone engaged.

In conversations with one individual, be it a lover, partner, or friend ensure that you are in direct contact primarily when they're talking. You should break your gaze at intervals of a couple of seconds, or more. Look upwards and towards one side and preferably to the left. This signals to the person you are talking to that you're trying to recall something, that will let them know as if you're seeking to enrich your conversation. It will also continue the conversation. Do not turn your back. This signifies an end of your conversation.

If you have to perform the majority of your listening for example, when you're an therapist or counselor, be careful not to make too eyes on one another, since the contact can make an uneasy person feel more fragile. Steven Atchison, an author of personal growth, suggests his method, which he calls the triangle. It is a method where you stare at the one eye for a few seconds, and then focus on your other eye for a couple of seconds and then turn your attention to your mouth for about a second and continue the rotation while the speaker speaks. Atchison is also adamant about nodding as well as using phrases of acceptance to demonstrate interest and make sure the speaker is speaking.

Eye contact may also help in winning an argument, without even saying a word. In a debate the direct contact with your eyes will make the opponent feel weaker and less powerful. This can confuse and irritate them and distracts your opponent from their argument. The way you look at your opponent throughout a debate at the same time they're talking and when you're speaking, is a sign of strength and trust. If someone is planning to provoke you, stay still and look directly at them. Do not look away. When you fail to do this, then you instantly end the discussion.

If you are looking to tell an individual that you appreciate you, make use of your eyes to look at the entire face of them. Pay attention to what they're talking about and respond with expressions like raised eyebrows or smiling. While doing this you should shift your focus between the eyes, face, their cheeks and even their mouth. In focusing on every aspect of the face, you keep eye contact, but not overpowering them with your constant focused gaze. It also shows that you have a keen interest in the different features that they have that translates into being fascinated by the different aspects of their character as well as their lives. The way you present yourself is you're interested in learning more about them, but without coming across as a desperate creepy stalker.

If you wish to show that you're more than just like someone you love, look up at the person. The extended eye contact may be the universal method to tell someone you love them, particularly when no words are required. Being able to engage in a silent, intimate eye contact can convey and increase feelings of love. It also increases connections between people so that you feel like they're having a intimate conversation that they only can comprehend.

The above strategies can help you build those kinds of trustworthy, friendly relationships that prosperous people around the globe depend on in order to achieve their ambitions. If you're timid or confident this approach will allow you to develop your technique for eye contact, and will make it the best tool to use for building strong relationships with your friends.

Chapter 6: Common Eye Contact Mistakes

We all know how important eye contact is in creating a lasting, positive first impression. But the fact that we are aware of how important it is does not make us more at ease with the process. Actually, it can make many of us concerned, which can lead to a greater sense of discomfort. There are some commonly-made eye contact errors every person should avoid, including people who are comfortable in establishing new relationships.

The biggest mistake that an individual can make when it comes to eye contact is approaching using it with assumption that everybody that you meet will be the same as your own. Many of us believe that we are conscious of differences, and which is why we recognize it. But the vast majority people also live every day with people who lead lives and have values which are

41

like the ones we have. It's a given that everybody else is the same as we do.

Keep our eyes on the fact that the globe is bursting with an array of different cultures and personalities in our lives are fueled through a global economy and globalization, it is inevitable to encounter someone with a life style, character as well as values are different those of our own. If you make eye contact, you should not think that because you consider it an act of respect and you're at ease with it, that the person with whom you are speaking will feel similarly. Instead, focus on the person you are talking to. When you learn the more you know about their personality, alter the way you use eye contact in line with this.

The main culprit is hyper-awareness of our most frequently made eye contact error. It is so difficult to demonstrate that we are aware of how important eye contact is that we often overuse it. When we attend job interviews, we are able to and look our interviewers directly in the eye all through the interview. On first dates, we sit and look directly into our partner's eyes throughout the meal from appetizer to dessert. A lot of eye contact whatever it is, can be just as unsettling, and perhaps more, as the absence of. If too much can give the impression that you are not confident in yourself or lack of interest when you are talking but too much can make you appear unsettling, frightening, and uncomfortable to look at. It is important to maintain a balance when making eye contact work at its best. Learning some of the methods that were discussed in earlier chapters can help you find this balance.

Self-confidence can be the root of the third most frequent mistake with eye contact. Everyone knows that when we

43

have to assume the leadership or present speeches the use of eye contact can convince our listeners or followers they are an entrusted expert on the topic that we are discussing. In contrast, focusing on our viewers all the time that you talk does not make them feel skilled, but it does make people feel snubbed. Maintaining a steady gaze when you talk is an effective strategy when you are trying to gain an edge over an equally ferocious opponent however, if you want your audience members to feel at ease at your table, going into attack approach will do exactly the opposite. The audience may be confused as to what you're doing to be insistent in trying to persuade them, and they'll be suspicious of your motivations as well as your honesty.

In truthfulness, or lack thereof, is the main reason behind another frequent eye contact error. Eye contact symbolizes honesty. Consequently in the event that we suspect that an individual is lying and we take a shifty glance as proof we're right. Most of the time honest people are aware of that and is likely to use excessive eye contact to fend off doubt. In the majority of cases, having greater eye contact doesn't necessarily mean that you are more honest.

In the same way having less contact with your eyes is not always a sign of lying. In the past, various individuals make eye contact in various methods. If we believe that anyone who is unable to look at their partner is lying, then we could also automatically consider any shy, introverted or socially anxious individual a lie-teller. This may seem absurd or extreme, however it proves that you need to take care when looking at the behavior of eye contact other people.

It is likely that our most commonly made eye contact errors have their the form of a common motif. These all stem in our inclination to miss interpret people who differ from us. It is a result of the desire to achieve efficiency in our assumptions of others by what we are aware about ourselves, our culture as well as our personality and our lives. If we're going to be able to benefit from the full effectiveness of eye contact and utilize it to help us and those around us, it's best to use this technique by taking our time. It is essential to take time to blend our knowledge of the individual or persons that are at issue with the information we have learned about the circumstance before us to determine the most effective method of using and understanding eye contact under any situation. In addition to a thorough understanding of the concept of eye contact it is also the best tool to build and sustaining positive, productive relationship.

Chapter 7: What Is Body Language?

That's where the path to mastering the art of body language begins. In the beginning by taking a moment to think and consider why you decided to further study body language? Do you think it was because you wish to be aware of the signals that your friend or family member exhibits? Perhaps, as I am is your fascination with the way people act and would like to know more about what and why. Whatever your reasons this chapter will present the fundamentals will help you master the art of body language. The fundamentals of body language are an entire overview of body language covering what it actually is (scientifically and of course) as well as how it operates within our relationships with other self, and the reasons why knowing the body language spoken by those in our lives is vital for our daily life. One of the principles I would like to impart with you is the fact that you are so much more than the physical bodies are a part of us. Each and every day, we communicate; the act of communicating is something that is a necessity. When we speak it isn't just using speech and words only. Also, we are using our tone, volume and even expression. It is true that communication can be both nonverbal as well as verbal. This is an interesting fact that I came across not so some time ago: "You've probably heard it said that most of what we communicate is accomplished through nonverbal methods: 93 percent, to be exact" (London Image Institute 2020). It is true that nonverbal communication can contribute significantly to the way we interact with other people. Our mouths are used to talk, but our bodies also talk. Everything from the way we stand or sit, to the colour of our clothing we put on all of our actions send an idea.

When we go through this text together, all the info provided will help you improve your ability to observe. If you want to become an expert of the body, it's essential that you are able to recognize the sign language while reading. As you progress through the book you'll notice that you develop your own unique style of watching. We'll now explore the forces that drive our curiosity in regards to understanding the body language. What do the forces behind at work behind the scenes?

Driving Forces Behind Body Language

What exactly is the meaning of body language? One of the best definitions of body language I've come across states that: "Body language is a silent orchestra in which individuals constantly reveal clues as to the things they're thinking or feeling. The body's movements and facial expressions, as well as volumes and vocal tone as well as other signs can be referred to collectively as body language" (Psychology Today, 2019,).

It is now time to ask which is what sparks curiosity about this idea? Many of us believe that there is a particular desire to discern when we're being misled that drives people to learn about non-verbal communications and body speech. For those who are more scientific who are among us, it's an attempt to better understand the body and how we communicate with it. There are many areas of curiosity all over the globe when it comes to the understanding of body language, and the various interest have combined to create an instructional manual for those of you. If I could have opinions on these issues I'd say that the most evident and persuasive reason for the movement toward understanding body language originates in the simple fact humans are sentient, and that sentient beings are naturally curious. So longer as we're aware that we are, we'll strive for understanding ourselves right down to the earliest cell that created us. This is, or we're only self-centered narcissists engulfed by our own desires! Pick your poison carefully. Spend a few moments reflecting on the reasons that brought you here. What enthralling aspect of you is calling you to learn how to communicate with your body and what is the reason? Hold on to that motivation to revert back to whenever you're not sure why you're in this particular journey. So, without further delay, let's get started with the fundamentals of body communication. We're ready to get started!

The Science of Body Language

If we are to consider the notion of body language and cut it into its simplest counterparts one of the primary and crucial components of the body language is the kinesics. It is a word you'll want to keep in mind and kinesics according to Lectera "studies nonverbal communication between people: how gestures, postures, facial expressions, the timbre of voice give away our true thoughts and intentions, even if we want to hide them" (Lectera 2021). Kinesics is divided in two groups: personal kinesics as well as culture-specific Kinesics. For personal kinesics, this term does not speak for itself. They are distinctive to you. They are not verbal and are a result of habits which you've built up through your entire life, because of the social discourse that has occurred within you throughout the years. Consider the cartoon characters, Bugs Bunny, and his famous practice of taking a bite out of his carrot, before asking, "What's up, Doc?" The positioning of one's hand beneath the elbow of the other while eating a carrot is an individual kinesic which we all identify as Bugs Bunny, even though it's an extremely typical non-verbal signal. In contrast the cultural kinesics can be fairly self-explanatory in that they're kinesics recognized and utilized by an entire society or even occasionally across the world (thanks to the online!). A good example of a culture-specific one can be observed within one hand motion that requires the person to place their forefinger and thumb with the form of an "L" on their forehead to signal that something or someone is considered to be a loser. The whole evolution of body language could be linked to kinesics and the two branches that comprise it. If you're keen to know more about the scientific basis behind kinesics help you immensely to go through the full text of Lectera's piece about the subject.

When it comes to the body language of a person There are lots of cultural differences to how we perceive the idea. The things you think is true and a fact in one village might mean little or nothing for the Amazonian tribe. Whatever you may perceive to represent a gesture that smacks that is negative or a sign of hatred, may be an expression that expresses love and appreciation elsewhere in the world! The kinesthetics of different cultures differ around all over the world The best method to understand that fact that you'll never be completely fluent in each one is to get familiar to the idea of communication across cultures. You'll be amazed at how understanding the basics of intercultural communication can ensure you never have ineffective difficulties with learning the art of body language across the globe. Although it may appear impossible at the moment yet, but tearing barriers between yourself and absorbing how the bodies of each person you come across is much easier accomplished than you think. Take

Indian cultures, for instance. In Indian society, it's common, and even expected to shake one's head while speaking. The gestures could include miniature gestures, shakes of the head, as well as tilts of the chin up as well as other. Although it's also a norm to be observed in English culture but the precise head movements Indian are known to use could convey an expression of body language that English people would normally be deemed offensive or rude however this isn't this case! When we learn the fundamentals of the various types of head gestures in Indian cultural practices, we are becoming more able to communicate with other cultures and move beyond the normal and into the unique.

So, with this thought in mind How do we dismantle these barriers? From a logical standpoint one of the things you'll need to practice the skills of observation. It's one thing know what non-verbal cues are, but it's quite another to know how to recognize their meaning at all! Also, understanding ways to hide your emotions as well as your emotional expressions during conversations with others is an art that is worthy of your time to master. One of the most important aspects to mastering the technique in body language involves disguising the fact that are an expert on the subject. No one would want to be a jerk who is looking at every movement they make during the course of a conversation. Your primary goal as an expert in body language should be to gather the data that you require while having an enjoyable, normal dialogue with the person that you're talking to.

Another important thing to keep in your mind during your journey is your mood and mental wellbeing. Being able to learn about the inside functioning of the minds of other people is that you are bound to discover something you'd rather not been aware of. It can cause a lot of harm for relationships with family members, close friends as well as close friends. It's important to be aware of when you should put a pause on doing your research and allow a truth be as the truth may result in more harm than beneficial (unless you are investigating a murder suspect, then it is essential to know the truth!).

Why Is Body Language Important?

Regarding the significance in body language can be accepted as a given that an knowledge of how we communicate through our bodies is essential in our modern world. Humans could perform and behave prior to speaking and communicate, which means that body language was developed before the development of verbal languages on an evolutionary scale. The language we use is the one that comes naturally to us and is what we turn repeatedly to communicate our ideas. Furthermore the body language is universally applicable and is able to be taught until you can speak it fluently in just a few hours, no regardless of where you go and the cultures you meet. This is the single and most effective method of communications across the world and to dismiss off body language as a second-rate alternative in comparison to speaking is absurdity by any measure. You aren't an stupid person! The reason why you're here. Simply put the importance of body language is as it helps us return to who we are as individuals We express our feelings in a more natural way by using body language with ourselves as well as to other people. A few of the most fundamental human actions are only possible to perform with the body. These include kissing, holding hands as well as hugging, dancing and kissing! These bodily actions encourage us and the people in our vicinity to connect and more in tune with the other.

In all I've outlined to you It is crucial to keep in mind that any situation where you look at and study the manner of speaking and body language used by the person you are talking to will yield outcomes solely based upon the context that is present in this exchange. Although working with a predetermined checklist of requirements may give some outcomes however, it will not offer the exact results you require. That's why being observant and able to mask your appearance are essential. By making sure you've got the fundamentals up to date, you are able to be absorbed in the situation that is in front of you, and continue striving to get maximum results by keeping your eyes on the specifics of the event that you are in. Maybe you're conducting an interview with a prospective employee of your organization, but it isn't clear if they're telling you what they really know about their previous experiences and abilities. This is why it will not help to know what they do with their lower part of their bodies as they'll likely be seated in a seat directly across from you or even on opposite sides of a monitor (again thank you internet!). However conducting an interview with the employee might necessitate you to concentrate on the signs of deceit and other signs that you might not be able to spot from your mother, for example. she relates the story of that lady at the grocery shop that her grandfather is always looking at when he believes that she's not there!

Common Idioms on Body Language Translated

In order to conclude this chapter, I'd be happy to provide you with a foundational understanding of a few words and phrases which are related to body language. This is a topic I'll use frequently throughout the book. "body language" itself is an idiom therefore if you're confused regarding what an idiom actually means, here is a great instance! A few other idioms which can be found within the notion of body language comprise:

"Spring" focus, or straight The expression refers to the situation where you've made someone completely and utterly immersed by what you're talking about which causes them to display that they are in a more focused posture. You might have caught them in the act of lying!

"To go "wall-eyed." It is the moment when a person's eyes expand or "bulge" in order to convey abrupt emotions, such as fear, anger, shock or even fear.

They are only a few of the many phrases you'll come across during the journey of body language. In order to make it simpler for readers, I've provided a glossary near the end of this guidebook that takes you through the latest body language. It is also mentioned throughout the book! Let's go to the next section, in which I will discuss the indicators that indicate that a person will communicate more through their body language as opposed to their voice.

Chapter 8: The Indicating Signs of Body Language

This chapter builds on of the basic. For us to learn to recognize the signals of body language in the most subtle way it is essential to understand the different ways that emotions manifest their emotions through physical gestures. The following chapter might seem insignificant to you, particularly if you grew up with open-minded people who were not afraid to reveal their real feelings as you grew older. This lesson, however, is important for anyone who has discovered that as they grew older people of power rarely expressed their feelings in gestures and so knowing the signals right from the start is worthwhile. Start at the top of the ladder and begin to work downwards.

Facial Expression

It is a given noting that the face is the main part of our body must be observed in order to determine what they're feeling and consequently depicting. The muscles in our faces that are responsible for creating and displaying facial expressions are called the craniofacial muscles, and there are over 20 of them in our faces (Clevelandclinic.org, 2022). They control our eyes, lips and cheeks. They also control the forehead nose and much more! They're rooted in the skull area that is the facial skeleton. This provides a base that we can work with when making facial expressions. When doing this, virtually all of them are utilized. Consider a moment to think about how you make your facial expressions when have a particular emotion; If you're feeling sad are you focused on what you do to show your sorrow with your facial expressions? It's a simple No. Our muscles of the craniofacial region are fine-tuned to the internal functions of the nervous system therefore, operate in a way that's impossible to control! We'll look at how our facial muscles produce diverse facial expressions according to the mood we are in.

Negative Emotions: Anger, Disgust, Fear, and Sadness

In observing a sour face expression of an person, it's important be aware of the eyes, nose the lips, the eyes and jaw. One of the most noticeable aspects of the expression is a collective twitching of the muscles that control the facial craniofacial area The eyebrows are drawn together and the eyes are narrowed. the lips may purse or part of them to expose teeth and then the jaw moves forward in a way that the lower row of teeth are overlapping the upper row. The eyes can widen or shrink depending upon the degree of rage an individual feels internal. If you observe a person's angry face expression, you'll observe an increase in wrinkles appearing on the surface of the face. It is due to them engaged and contracting a large amount of their facial muscles due to the stress and frustration that they feel on the inside. The jutting and baring of the teeth are directly influenced by human evolution, as well as the fact that teeth were the primary defense mechanism in the past, prior to the advent of old-fashioned weapons (Parvez 2020).

Parvez (2021) says that disgust and anger can frequently be misinterpreted as them due to their similarities. Both utilize similar facial muscles and each cause wrinkles to the face as a whole. The major differences worth looking for in trying to detect disgust an angry mood are the patterns caused by the eyes, nose and the cheeks. If someone is feeling anger, rather than burning their nostrils and snorting, they'll pull the nostrils straight upwards, causing lines of wrinkles appear across that bridge that connects the eyes. Eyes can become small to the degree that they look nearly shut (a useful way of determining the degree of a person's disgust in this instance is to determine how wide the eyes appear) as well as the neck may pull towards the neck, it's as if the individual wants to physically pull away from the the conversation, which has made the person to be disgusted (Parvez 2021).

On the next list of facial expressions that are negative is fear. It is simple to distinguish from disgust and anger because although these two feelings frequently complement each other however, fear is distinct emotion that is usually related to shock or uncertainty. If we're afraid the eyebrows, instead of sweeping upwards, as they do in anger, they will rise high across the forehead. They'll then tuck them in making fewer wrinkles on the hairline and brow. The eyes expand dramatically and show more white when we're angered or discontented. Based on Parvez (2015) the reason for this is due to the fact that our instinctual selves scan the surroundings to identify a threat could require us to fight back against. In the most extreme circumstances, the jawline and the lips may become taken back in a similar manner as when we express our displeasure. It is crucial to look at the face expressions of a person at a holistic level in order to understand their feelings.

The emotion of sadness is among the toughest feelings to identify for an individual. Consider this: what else could cause suicide rates to be that high? If we could discern the indications of depression and sadness among the people around us, and especially those we love dearly, treatment and therapies for people experiencing extreme sadness would prove to be more efficient. Although sadness can be difficult to recognize in the present however, it is possible to recognize subtle signs of how someone is experiencing by looking at their eyelids, lips and eyes. Eyebrows can be tipped towards the middle while the lips could be turned downwards towards the corners and create an upside-down "U for the cheeks. If someone is unhappy, they're more inclined to gaze downwards, revealing an increased eyelid area. Some other indicators are red eyes with glassy lenses and bloodshot skin (Parvez 2022). Always approach the person if they're showing sadness with their expressions even if doing it without thinking about it!

Positive Emotions: Happiness and Surprise

After we've got all our negative feelings out of the picture, let's move toward positive emotions! Did you ever hear of the expression, "It takes 43 muscles to frown and only 17 to smile"? The phrase has been cited by numerous scholars and researchers in the past mostly due to its being factual. The term "happy" is utilized as an umbrella term that covers the broad and virtually endless spectrum of emotions related to positivity because it is true that when you feel positive it means that we're satisfied. An expression of happiness on the face shows the lips turned upwards (i.e. smiles!) and can be shaved off to reveal teeth. The eye's corners are also inclined upwards which causes 'crow's foot' or talon-shaped wrinkles, that appear in front of the eyes. Eyebrows are usually unaffected when someone smiles or displays happiness in the event that it is more powerful, like laughing or shock. If a person is content there are less wrinkles on the smooth, supple skin on their face.

In the opposite it is commonplace to associate surprise with joy. But, it should not be taken as a fact. The emotion of surprise must be regarded as the bridge between positive and negative. It is due to the fact that in the event that someone is shocked when they're confronted with an event that is completely unexpected for the person. The brain of their cognitive system didn't anticipate being confronted by this event which is why they're uncertain of how they should respond. This is where the phrase "blank expression" originates. Eyes may open slightly, and mouths may be able to become open. However, generally speaking the skin on the face does not show wrinkles, with the exception for the normal wrinkles. It is a feeling which you need to pay attentively to during your quest to learn your body speech! In a brief moment, you can choose in between the positive and negative feelings You have the chance to examine the reactions of your partner in conversation before they have the chance to control their own emotions.

Posture

Posture can reveal something about the intensity of an individual's fascination with you and the topic of conversation. This is a different idiom that can help the subject: Posture refers to how we carry our bodies. That is to say, our posture is our own mental or physical outward display of our behavioral attitude at the time of display (merriam-webster.com, 2019). It is a notion that must be considered to be very contextual in any circumstance, since it could be altered at will as well as on the basis of. In order to keep it simple but to be more precise, we're going to examine posture from a simple perspective, i.e. the way it's presented within a normal, controlled setting. It includes the position of our arms and torsos, an internal idea known as'space zones', the gestures we make with our hands, as well as our foot placement. Signs that tell you something about an individual's posture could reveal numerous hidden emotions, including tension, anxiety, and deceit. We'll take a look at all of these sections of posture more depth, so you'll be able to recognize them and look at them from a different perspective.

Arm Position

The most well-known arm posture that is a favorite among expert body language specialists is made up of arms folded, either in front or behind. Arms are folded in a variety of ways along the front of your body. They could be folded in a tight manner over the chest, loosely on the stomach or crossed by the wrists front of the abdominal region (Taylor 2021). In the same way, arms may be folded back behind the back. In this case, an person grasps the wrist opposite by using one hand in order to extend the chest slightly. Arms folded in this manner, similar to position, can be highly context-specific in that an identical arm posture may have both negative and positive implications, based upon the context. In addition to having the arms folded over your body, the arms could change into different forms including hands resting upon the hips, creating large triangles that are open on both sides of the body. There is also arms being positioned towards a person who is speaking to them (perhaps as pointed accusatory gestures). In the next chapter, we'll be examining the way that arms communicate the intent of a person and how to study the movement of arms and their positioning for clues like deceit and aggression.

Space Zones

Space zones can be explained quite easily. They refer to what is accepted as a reasonable distance between people from any society. For instance, in the United States, an acceptable space-zone is thought to be anywhere between 12 and 15 inches. This is a variable between the different cultures (iimn.org 2016). This is the reason it's crucial to learn the kinesthetics and cultural background of those you'll be studying to avoid the chance of making the wrong assumption which could cause a rift in your research! After the cultural kinesics have been cleared from the equation they can be utilized to discern the motives of the person whom you're talking to. In particular, those who lie tend to distance themselves towards the person they attempt to deceive (although it isn't always the situation).

Hand Gestures

In addition to everything we've been discussing one of the most crucial body parts that we should pay attention to in analyzing body language are hand and foot. Hands are used to complete a variety of tasks in daily life, from taking care of us, to cooking and driving, all the way to highlighting an idea in a the conversation. Hands and fingers and the manner in which people utilize their hands to communicate, can frequently be among the most trustworthy aspects of body speech when it comes down to understanding someone's individual Kinesiology. The majority of unconscious ideas and thoughts are revealed by the movements of hands, largely due to the fact that they are frequently used throughout the day. The more roles the body organ performs as a body part, the more unconscious actions are performed by the body component. Hand gestures (and fingers and hands generally) are closely connected to power dynamics within the field of analysis of body language. Particularly, we utilize the hands to demonstrate the power and authority (or contrary) during conversations with people we do not know well. Through this guide it will be clear how keeping an eye on the hand movements of a person when you begin the conversation is crucial in creating the strength interaction between you over the remainder of your discussion.

Foot Placement

Finally, in terms of body posture and foot position, we also have the issue of foot placement. Parvez (2015b) will bring us back into the full circle in his discussion of foot position in relation to body communication. In the main, the positioning of one's feet in chat will inform us most about the location, and towards whom the focus of their attention goes. Also what direction the feet of a person are pointed while they're talking to you (unless they are controlled in any way by the person) will reveal more about where their attention is traveling than any other aspect or body part!

The chapter is focusing mostly on educating you to the various body parts and the role they perform in observing body language In Chapter 3, we will dive into the fundamentals of body language, particularly as it pertains to conversations as well as interaction between strangers. In addition, the next chapter will offer the broad spectrum of power dynamics as well as ways to evaluate the various purposes your friend or colleague might convey through body communication.

Chapter 9: Body Language Facts You Can Use

If you've got the fundamental skills required to evaluate an individual's body language you should learn how to judge the individual's intent towards you. This chapter is intended to equip you with the necessary tools that will help you analyze the body language of your partner in conversation. Be aware however that the majority of analyses you conduct based on these strategies are made in the initial stages of the conversation i.e beginning in the first part! Imagine it as an actual boxing match (although I hope that you won't be engaged in physical combat at anytime) The first few rounds will be focused on getting acquainted with your adversaries. What is their swing? Which parts of your body do they call for attention as you talk?

How to Pick Up the Signals

In a way that is as simple as it is possible, figuring out how to detect signs in a person's body language that they're using to communicate what they want to convey through the use of non-verbal signals - takes time and effort. Beginning it is essential to be aware and alert, however with time, you'll observe a significant improvement in your understanding of the body language of people who are around you. Common cues start to be revealed in your subconscious mind and then, you'll be taught to dig deeper into subtle signals that provide you with the information you require to know.

First thing be looking for is whether the person you are talking to is open to sharing their thoughts with you. Anyone who is eager to have an open and genuine conversation will be able to keep the feet pointing at you, and they will usually appear more comfortable. However those who aren't eager to share their thoughts might even go so far as to keep their arms and legs placed over each other so as to guard their body's unconscious from sharing too much.

If you want to recognize those signs that indicate lying and truth The best method to use when analysing the body language of your companion is to search at the lack of truth rather than any indication of falsehood. When we lie, it is because we try to trick our brain to believe things that haven't happened. It is not possible to fool ourselves! The brain is able to come up with a method to argue with us. This could may be through a subtle shaking at the head in lieu of accepting, or gesture of a toe towards the opposite direction from what was is intended (Navarro and Schafer 2001). Also, if someone lies about us verbally and their body will discover an opportunity to tell us that they're not so open to discussion as they would like us to be.

The process of identifying deceit when a person is conversing has a lot to do with figuring out the presence of someone who is and/or against you during the conversation. If you're not engaged in an actual argument, knowing the truth can be a challenge! It is for this reason that Navarro as well as Schafer (2001) instruct that we should focus on an individual's eyes in order to judge the degree to which they agree with our views. A more frequent or prolonged blink could indicate disagreement, or even dishonesty (Navarro and Schafer 2001). In the same way, regular and controlled blinks that are executed in a steady pattern suggests that the individual who you're speaking with is completely engaged in the topic you're talking about and is largely in agreement with your opinions. communicating.

In addition to all this aside from all of this, one of the main things that you must determine in the earliest possible time in any interaction is who the authority rests. The fact is, at the end day, humans are a species of hierarchy This characteristic can be found in everything we do including entire nations down to conversations between two individuals. If you are trying to determine the dynamics of power during your interactions, watch for signs like bent arms, a straight posture, an extended stance as well as intense eye contact. On the other hand, an obvious indication that someone whom you're talking to has assumed the character as a submissive chatterboxer is in their eyes. Are they trying to avoid eye contact with their eyes by turning down or away?

Eye contact, in addition, will tell us more about how committed someone has to a particular interaction. Navarro as well as Schafer (2001) guide us through the factors that make people seem to be interested in a conversation such as sitting forward or yawning at specific statements or the increased utilization of facial expressions natural to them. You can utilize this information to identify when the person we are talking to could pay attention to the words we're using! They might be reclined back in their seat, struggling to keep their eyes on us, as they take in deeper breaths or cross their arms over their chests. This is a sign of a person who isn't interested to talk with us and may prefer to be somewhere else (rude!).

Tips on How to Use Body Language to Your Advantage

Once you are able to recognize the signals of non-verbal signals, you should learn ways to apply the information to benefit you. Understanding the body language of others is one thing but understanding how you can control the body language of your own in order to alter a situation completely different! This is especially important situations where we need to gather details from someone, or maybe they've committed an act of violence and we're the ones investigating. If this happens what we do and establish an atmosphere of power is vital as it determines where we would like the conversation to be.

Everyone hates to be the one who is a victim. Particularly when looking to influence an interaction in order to satisfy our personal requirements, making ourselves the primary participant within the discussion is an inescapable fact. Make sure you're confident by expanding your posture if you are standing or crossing your knees on top of the other in a sitting position. Additionally, you should use your hands! Navarro as well as Schafer (2001) are insistent on the traditional Mr. Burns hand gesture that involves the points of each finger are positioned together to create an illusion of expectation and strength. A different example of power in a conversation is the bending of the hands downwards to demonstrate force on another. It is easy to explain but with some insight into the reasons behind it. Think about meditation for instance. "When upward palms are used in mediation, they position both the mind and the body in an open posture that enhances listening" (Phillips and Radish, 2011). But the thing is that we do not want to be listening! We want our partner to be able to feel a subconscious desire to pay attention to us to get the results we desire from them.

It is also crucial to keep in mind that we can't rely solely on the non-verbal clues to achieve what we desire! Human bodies are an extremely well-oiled (unless you're not moisturizing) machine. We function better when all the components of our body are together. When you're controlling your conversation, make sure you are combining the non-verbal and verbal signals carefully. A lot of this will come easily to you when you build confidence with time. However, initially it's important to learn the common phrases that are appropriate with certain non-verbal signals to highlight the degree of control you have over your counterpart in the conversation.

That being said It is crucial to be aware that you should use your power to do the good and not for evil. In order to do that it is essential to earn respect from those in your life and those who you are in contact with. If you are learning to mold the spoken and non-spoken signals and of course paying attention to the particular context of the scenario you're currently performing in, speaking and acting first will yield most effective outcomes. The waiting around to speak or perform is only going to diminish the trust others place on them! People tend to trust and admire anyone who's not afraid to be heard, has quick and powerful leadership abilities and creates an impression of not just playing. This is particularly useful in interviews or business gatherings.

But, these techniques would not be useful without an understanding of the public. What is your ideal interlocutors like? Do you know the general atmosphere in the room from your own head? If you want to be successful in the game of power-play the player must be able to anticipate what your guests will feel to certain events. You can assess the deliberation of your crowd by performing one quick sweep through the area before the game commences, and examining every facial expression for signs of emotion such as happiness, anger or anger. Look at the facial features! This type of understanding is applicable to rhythm and timing as well. The act of preparing yourself prior to the start of a meeting (a business meeting such as a meeting at a corporate office) will be enough to allow you to hit the start. The key is to ensure that you keep your pace throughout the length of the interaction by studying the expressions of the audience and the pace of the conversation. A tip to avoid: launching into a lengthy negotiation when your guests are already getting ready to take a break might not be the most appropriate time. Examine their body language to determine if they are interested. Are they engaged? Invested? Are they moving their arms, and then reclined their chairs? Once you're sure that your audience is paying attention to you with the complete focus of the audience then it's the time to put back in the game your dynamic. Keep the momentum going by using the scenario of a business meeting. You might have to present an investment of a million dollars to the directors of your company. The board has seen these before. What does it make you unique? First you are able to read them just like books, which means you're aware of the key entrances into the psyches of their subjects are. Watch for the moment that your body's collective signals signal that they are paying attention, then add your power play. One of the best ways to accomplish this, particularly when you're speaking in an event such as this, is to extend your posture.

You have now drew the full attention of your public (with the most brilliant concept, whatever that might be) you must ensure that you don't allow yourself to get caught up in the excitement and romance of your tale. Human brains can struggle to process and process large quantities of information that are complex at once, which is why it's crucial to incorporate a few intriguing stories into your story. In order to get back in the game, you have to (literally) make a move back. It will allow your audience space to digest what they've learned so far. It will also give an opportunity to cement your message in their heads through an example that allows the audience to connect the information they've learned by using a concrete scenario.

The time has come for coffee! If you've got perfectly, the audience is likely to gravitate towards needing an interruption. In addition, being able to give them a break at precisely the right moment will signal to your guests that you're in sync with the atmosphere of the space, and you know their needs. The act of offering refreshments (in the case of some, having the refreshments you provide your own) can help create an impression of trust between your host and the person you are speaking to. Navarro & Schafer (2001) confirms my assertion on this issue. As special agents in the FBI They frequently employed the method of refreshment to reduce tension within the interrogation area.

One of the essential body language tricks you can apply to help you when communicating with others is shaking hands. Even though it is true that the Western manner of greeting hands with a stranger might differ from one another all across the globe however, nearly every single culture of our time has a form of farewell or greeting which involves touching hands. Handshakes with the person you're speaking with prior to a meeting might be exactly what makes a difference in the instant relationship between you two, allowing an advantage you may have not realized you required.

Confident Body Language - The Dos and the Don'ts

There are a variety of methods to show that you are an assertive person by the way you speak, however it's crucial to consider that the context in every situation can determine whether or not it will be a success for your self-confidence. Being aware of the power dynamics of any conversation will let you know whether it is appropriate to show confidence and also the times when it's not an appropriate time to do so.

The Do's

Whatever way you are over your partner in conversation, be sure that you must work hard to maintain the trust level between the two of you. Make sure to keep a break for coffee in your mind, but try not to smile too often! Your primary goal towards the end of your day is to establish an environment that is positive in the group, so that everybody feels at ease and comfortable in their place within the discussion.

The Don'ts

In this way It can be difficult at times to be caught up in the sense of power and accomplishment that winning an argument brings. Be a person who is determined to keep their self-esteem under control at all times regardless of who you're talking to. Be careful not to let confidence overflow your mind with air! Although saturating your conversation partner with a dominant body language could work, you'll eventually lose their respect and trust. they might choose to share less to you due to this. The moral of the story is Be a good leader.

The chapter might have seemed as a long time, but understanding how to communicate your body language with a manner that gives your desired results is essential when learning your body communication. In the next chapter we'll dive in a bit more deeply into how you can let your own body language work and the way that body language functions overall. We'll get science-based!

Chapter 10: How Body Language Works & How to Make Your Body Language Work for You

To continue from the last chapter, we'll examine a greater depth at ways to help your body language to work for you in all kinds of environment. Although it may be complicated, but it's essential to be aware of ourselves prior to when trying to get to know other people and there's nothing more embarrassing than a person making assumption about subjects that they are nothing about! In this section we'll look at the congruity and incongruity with ourselves and also hiding, studying our behavior, as well as some helpful tips on how to improve the way you communicate the non-verbal signals you use. Let's begin.

Guide to Congruence

The first question is how do you define what is congruence? What on Earth do you mean by congruence what does it mean? It is said that according the work of Trout as well as Rosenfeld, "The postures of two interactants can be said to be congruent when the interactants hold their bodies, especially their extremities (heads, arms, hands, legs, and feet), in the same position as each other" (Trout and Rosenfeld in 1980, p.177). Also, to remain in a congruous position with the person we are talking to means we're to some extent reflecting their non-verbal signals. In the majority of cases it is the case that congruence within our everyday interaction is completely natural and to the point that it is often difficult to recognize it's taking place. In this regard whenever we wish to convince someone we're in a natural accord with them about a certain issue, knowing how to intentionally mirror what they are saying could prove to be a valuable ability.

Tips on How to Look Congruent

When we have to appear in concord with the other person in conversation being aware of the non-verbal signals to mimic should be at the top of our checklist of things to consider. The appropriate balance between being in agreement with a person but maintaining an advantage in terms of the power dynamics that are in play may be a challenge however it should not put your off. When you encounter these situations regardless of the position you're in, whether sitting or standing, you should try to keep a consistent focus on your lower part of your friend. The lower portion of your body is able to communicate with the subconscious mind a amount when we focus on keeping the same body language creating an invisible bond of trust and not letting ourselves be swayed. If the person you are talking to isn't well-versed in the body's language that you (and don't underestimate their abilities!) The likelihood of them seeing the perfect mirroring of your body language is very slim.

Guide to Incongruence

However it is inevitable that there will be instances in your life when being in a constant conversation with a person isn't feasible because of a variety of various circumstances. If this occurs and your plan fails, it's essential not to put yourself in the blame. There are many causes for that we may not be able to "feel the way we want to with our partners in the way we'd like to. For a first time date, to take an instance. Perhaps you've matched up with one of your friends on Tinder whom, at first glance, looks to be perfect! The two of you get along well on messages, but when you go out for dinner with your partner and you realize that the uncomfortableness can't be ignored. How you wish you could understand the way your body speaks in order to ease the mood and begin to meet your companion...

How to Avoid Incongruence

Here's the answer. The first step is to acknowledge that you won't know who you're interacting with regardless of the effort you put into. Sometimes, they're adept at masked communication (which we'll be learning more about in the next section). If this happens instead of focusing all your attention to mirror your persona focus it toward avoiding inconsistency. Both of these things might sound similar, but when you're in the middle of a conversation when you start to feel like everything is beginning to slide down the slope, trying to avoid disaster in order to stay in the right direction may be your only alternative. This is especially the case in circumstances that are at risk of becoming violent, or during an encounter where one party is extremely dominant. Watch out for indicators such as an increase in the power of play, and then react by muting similar signals. Be careful not to appear insensitive, which could make the other person feel uncomfortable.

Guide to Over Congruence

The other side of the spectrum, from complete discord, we can have the concept of congruity. It is indeed possible to appear out of sync with your partner in conversation! In the end, at the time our primary goal in studying the behavior of an person is to conduct the analysis with a manner that is discrete and not noticeable. Nobody wants to discover that they're the object of your own personal research which they didn't accept, even though they thought they were taking a break to discuss their relationship with an ex. In the rush to make our non-verbal cues clear and body language, we tend to forget the obviousness of our body. Reflecting every non-verbal signal which your partner in conversation emits is likely cause them to be aware about the reality that they are mirroring them and leading them to suspect of something being afoul.

How to Avoid Over Congruence

Another way of solving this type of problem is to avoid. First, it is important to not get to the point of miscongruity immediately. Inducing doubt in the interaction can lead to catastrophe, as it can cause your to be on the fragile line between resolving the issue and total disintegration of confidence. In order to avoid confusion ensure that you have three or four clues that are not verbal within your mind to take advantage of when you find your mind wandering. It could be a stinging sensation on your nostril, or swishing the fingers over the hair or switching the cross-legs of your knees. Naturally, it's essential to check that the person you are talking to doesn't do the same too!

Guide to Masking

If we're observing the expressions of another It is easy to overlook the fact that they could possess some or all our knowledge in interpreting non-verbal signals. In this regard, you should never overestimate the person whom you interact with. they might have been reading this book as well! If you're looking to shield yourself from the criticism of the people who try to evaluate your own self, it's worthwhile to learn to cover the most basic elements of your body that may expose you to suspicion. These could include the way you hold your hands, posture and foot position, as well as the movement of your head. If we cover up our non-verbal communication that way, we're in a way, protecting us from what our conversationsal other party might say or do depending on their perception of the way we communicate.

How to Mask Effectively

Masking is a process that requires effort and time and is often an experiment with trial and error. Additionally, masking your body language is highly congruous and is largely based on the impressions that are given to you by your contact. In the case of example, if your person with whom you're speaking to seems withdrawn, uninterested or unwilling to divulge many details it is a sign that they're aware of interactions that are taking place and have a desire to not be viewed as the weaker side. To come out in the top position, you have be able to hide your feelings and your non-verbal signals at a level that matches or surpasses the other person's, while also looking at what they give to you. This can be accomplished by following the guidelines in the earlier chapter on showing dominance and strength. If you are trying to hide your body language naturally It's important to recognize the unease (and perhaps, even anxiety) that the person creating in you, and to identify the non-verbal aspects of your body that could be showing this discomfort and then be in control of those parts to ensure that they do not reveal any information.

Your Verbal vs. Nonverbal Skills

Being in control of your body language is just one aspect of the fight However, there is more to it. Navarro and Schafer, who are our trusty FBI agents, have told us that the true way to succeed in analysing someone's behavior is an overall observation of the verbal and non-verbal signals (Navarro Schafer and Schafer 2001). I strongly suggest reading the entire article in order to gain an understanding of what kind of signals people tend to emit during certain scenarios. For this particular instance we'll be focusing on you and your language capabilities in conjunction with the non-verbal skills you possess. The process of understanding your individual skills requires a significant amount of self-reflection and time however, the majority of the process is realizing and acknowledging parts of you that existed already. Take a recording of yourself engaging in an informal conversation with your loved ones regarding something trivial or trivial, then listen to notice the specific phrases and words you may utilize more often than others. If you compare these words with the terms Navarro and Schafer discuss in their piece and you'll learn more regarding how you speak when speaking.

Analyzing and Evaluating Your Own First Impressions

In the context of analysing yourself, one thing that I'm sure that we all undertake regardless of the setting of the situation is to analyze what we can learn from our initial impressions we've created on the people around us. There is no doubt that I am not the only one to have been unable to leave an initial conversation thinking "Gosh what did I say? make that comment? !" While it is crucial to think about the way we communicate with others when we first meet them however, it's equally important not to judge us. Understanding the body language of others doesn't have to mean getting the desired results from individuals (although this is certainly a big benefit!) Many of us simply want to develop our social skills. If you take everything you've learnt so far and applying it to the initial impressions that you create and you'll be able to come away of every interaction by analyzing what the other person's reaction was at certain words you spoke or did.

Practical Steps to the Perfect Body Language Performance

Additionally, by studying the non-verbal signals you observed and interpreted in relation with one another You will then be able to return to the second session using all the cards that you hold! You might be asking why do I on Earth do I present the best performance of my own life if I'm not acting? First, you need to consider is that the world isn't a stage and you'll be amazed by how easily certain body language components appear with a goal to think about. We'll now look at the three actions you should follow to improve the quality of your non-verbal communication regardless of the situation.

Step One: Know Your Goal(s)

You should have your goal or goals set. What are you hoping to accomplish from this conversation? Are you the first or the second time you'll be in contact with this individual How often are you planning to meet them in the near future? Is it possible that the person lies to you or perhaps concealing something? It is not a good idea getting into a confrontation using all these methods for understanding people but not having a clear idea of what you wish to discover. Yes, there are situations in which people engage in conversations with others simply for the fun of it, however in the majority of cases all of our interactions serve a reason, and understanding what that is is the very first step towards success.

Step Two: Play to Your Strengths

After you have your principal target or goal written down within your head then it's time to choose which instruments you will employ from your toolbox to achieve your target. In the case of, say, if you're conversing with a person who you think is lying about you (perhaps the person you are with whom believes is committing fraud) You are likely to open up your box of tools that contain all the elements needed to spot deceit within that person. It is not a good idea to show at a gunfight wearing knives! Understanding the tools you're likely to require comes with understanding the tool you will use the best. Are you unsure of what skills you are proficient in? Do your best in all of it.

Step Three: How to Work Through Body Language Change

Keep this in mind when you are making decisions You must also be flexible to any changes in the way you communicate with your partners. In the past the context for each situation that you are in will determine how you decide which signs to look for and when to behave. The topic of conversation could occur that irritates your partner, leading the person to withdraw into their own and create non-verbal barriers between yourself and them. Be aware of the changes in your non-verbal behaviour will enable you understand the motivations of the person you are talking to. In addition, it will assist you to determine what strategies are effective; maybe you should consider a change?

In this chapter, we examined various ways to learn about your body language i.e. the personal Kinesics. We also discussed ways to help our own kinesics do the do the work for us, such as the ability to manage their nuances to a certain degree in order to shield our self from being vulnerable in front of others (especially people who are aware of more than us about the non-verbal clues!). Moving on to our next chapter, which we'll explore the way that body language varies among genders and different cultures across the globe.

Chapter 11: The Different Body Languages

As we begin to kick the chapter I feel it's essential to tackle a problem which may be occupying your thoughts when you think of gender, and the associated body language. I want to emphasize that in the context in this chapter I'll teach you typical non-verbal signals that are related to the two primary genders: both female and male. This isn't my goal to exclude anyone from my classes, so I've crafted this chapter to a degree which allows you to read the text according to your gender preference and pronouns. We be in agreement that there exist certain signs that don't speak between the sexes regardless of specific body parts that one is able to possess and another and does not have, or any other factors! While not getting too caught up in the nuances of politics we can look into the gender implications of body communication.

The Gender (Body) Language

There are no doubts that there are certain elements of body language used more frequently from one sexual sexe over one. One example and widely known fact regarding flirting between sexes is that it involves the female part of "batting" the eyelashes whenever flirtatious interest is wanted. It is perfectly normal for males to take advantage of this cue that is not verbal however, it's a universally seen with females, so it is a situation that will require us to understand why a male does this. Another example is of the masculine role of making a knee-high gesture while proposing to a woman partner. This isn't normal, but it's widely accepted because of the influence of history and tradition that have shaped modern society. However, I would suggest that you constantly question the gender roles of society, to challenge the status quo, I believe that it's important to know the fundamental beliefs of institutions that each of us has ingrained within the majority of us. Some of these ideas have been instilled so deeply into our minds that we have a tendency to accept them without conscious thought even today. Let's begin with women and then look at the subtle cues that have been attributed to these genders.

Body Language for Her

Michael Arangua over at Better Help provides us with a fascinating understanding of female body language. He specifically focuses on the unjust and destructive expectations that our women face because of their discriminatory past.

According to Arangua Although women may present themselves "as such" to you but her body language frequently "tell the tale" of the way she feels (Arangua 2022a). In the background, issues of dominance will always remain at the top of women's minds especially when she is talking with men. So whenever we're watching and studying the manner in which women communicate Our primary objective should be to search for indications of what our modern-day wealthy white men call "submission," or lack of.

Facial Expression

The face is the first thing we'll look at. Arangua informs us that females are more likely to smile and sigh significantly more than males (Arangua 2022a). For no reason or their own, they have a history and its impact on women in the

119

present has created an unconscious and unhealthy pressure to relax. The past was a time when women were denied rights and were less oppressed, it was not their right to assert their rights or debate about any subject. Bessel Van der Kolk's fascinating research-based memoir about trauma, called The Body keeps the score, gives us a myriad of details regarding generational trauma and how it may take many forms and pass down via the psyches of generations (Van Der Kolk, 2015.). For women who have suffered from trauma, it has been transmitted via their body speech. This is why they generally smile and nod in response to various emotions. They also do this the time they're hiding particular emotions also. This being said the next time you meet someone, be attentive to her happiness! It is possible that she's not as keen as she's telling you.

Proximity

Then, moving to the concept of proximity (i.e. spaces zones) Let's look at the ways women interact with individuals through the way they manage the people they are close to. In the article, Arangua emphasizes one certain feature of body language used by women which is being leaning towards the front (Arangua 2022a). Studies show that women are more likely to utilize the act of leaning (or refusing to lean) towards the front and back in order in order to convey their concern for their companion within a particular situation. The context of the conversation is crucial when it comes to this. As we're dealing with the subject of gender, there is no doubt that flirting could be a factor when it comes to a particular situation. If you're considering this article as someone who wants to meet ladies romantically, it's crucial to not assume that women are looking for romance in you by leaning forward in conversations. Leaning forward for women, usually indicates that they are interested in the conversation you're having. In contrast being leaning back can mean that the reverse is true, and perhaps you should change the conversation topic.

Touching

When it comes to the way women interact via touch, Arangua instructs that we should concentrate on the technique handshakes. He says that the way the woman shakes her hand will tell you lots about how she feels about her, how engaged she is with the relationship and also her feelings about the dynamics of power in play. The answer is simple in the end. Handshakes that are weak can indicate an absence of enthusiasm and a lack of control over strength dynamics, or even anxiousness. On the other hand, a firm one could indicate confidence, power, and power (Arangua 2022a). Consider what we've learned so far, specifically when it comes to shaking hands. As I said before, you should shake hands prior to and after an encounter regardless of what the interactions might involve (of of course, if you go to the grocery store it is not necessary to shake hands with cashiers prior to and following the exchange of the cash). While analyzing the facial expressions of a woman, you can try looking at the intensity of her handshakes prior to and after you have spoken to her. It might get stronger as more time she spends with your personality, and weaker in the event that she didn't receive what she expected from the interaction.

Body Language for Him

As we move on to the next subject we'll cover in this book, we'll explore males. In this case we will allow Arangua to guide us by the arm with male non-verbal signals, like he did for females. According to Arangua "the body language of men can be easy to read if you know what you are looking for" (Arangua 2022b). The reason for this is that males are thought to be less complicated in general as they emit the least complex set of non-verbal messages. It may be simpler to read males than women, it's important to remember that males communicate using the different body parts as women do. We'll take a deeper study of how (not as much about the reason!).

Facial Expression

While observing facial expressions and gestures of men in the form of his face instead of taking note of how often the man smiles or nods the most important thing is to pay attention and study his gaze and eyes, and also the subtle smiles his eyes may make during the course of an encounter. First, you're going be able to pay attention to the frequency and speed of the blinks. If you notice that a person seems to blink more quickly than average (or fast enough to make you can tell) This could indicate that he's stressed or anxious. Based on the circumstances of the event, this can be a result of a range of different causes. A different aspect of men's eyes you need to pay attention to is the direction in which it's focused in conversation especially when you're talking. An eye that is focused towards the lower part of your face as you're speaking indicates you are listening and inhaling what you're speaking (Arangua 2022b, arangua).

Proximity

If you're a total novice when it comes to knowing the body language of males, then you could be in the same boat with many people across the globe because you may believe in this popular legend: If a man minimizes his personal space or enters into the space of the person he's communicating with, it implies that he's trying to intimidate of the person so that he can gain some advantage in the exchange. As per Arangua isn't accurate! The research shows that people who decrease the contact between themselves with the person they're communicating with actually feel at a disadvantage or intimidated by the person. Hence, cutting down on their proximity can be a way to "take up as little space as possible" (Arangua, 2022b). However, this unlikely to be an issue in the context of romance. In any case, moment you're talking with a guy (in an informal setting) and he decides to take an involuntary step toward the other person, he's subconsciously losing a little bit of the power he has in the discussion due to the non-verbal signals you give him!

Touching

Additionally, lots could be discussed about men through his physical interactions with the people around him. Handshakes are a common topic in the male setting. It is vital to note that, even though research suggests that women do not pay thought to what meanings their gestures might convey to the others, the act of handshakes is one which men tend to think about frequently due to traditions and the expectations of society. Particularly, males prefer to focus their attention in the force of their grips on another individual's hand. In this regard whenever you shake a man's hand, take note of the way he holds the one you are holding. One might want to establish a energy dynamic with a tense handshake. However, one that's too firm may suggest that he's striving too hard, and could make things worse than he planned completely (Arangua 2022b). Similar to the approach I recommended that you do when making a handshake with a female Try comparing the force of a man's handshake both before and after your interaction with him to determine how your interaction took place, and how the man is feeling after the interaction has concluded.

The Culture (Body) Language

Apart from the way we see body language within the context of both genders and age group, there's a lot to discuss about how people generally consider body language when is related to the different diverse cultures across the globe. Understanding how to understand and align with body language unique to your cultural background is like a stroll in the park when compared with studying the same when is applicable to the cultural tradition you're not familiar with. Given the rate that globalization is spreading across the globe and transforming the world, you'll be interacting daily with different cultures throughout your time! This is why it's essential to know the basic concepts of intercultural communication the sense of non-verbal communication. To comprehend this concept more clearly, read of Oberg's famous essay about the idea of culture shock, and its different phases; you may be surprised to discover that you resemble it far more than you anticipated (Oberg 1960). For an easy way for you to understand the various stages of culture shock can be seen on a diagram in a U-shape to symbolize the challenges we have to face as we attempt to integrate into the culture of a different one. In the final phase, we must master which for you signifies mastery over the cultural language!

Geography

The body language of a culture changes as you travel. It's common to overlook the fact that in the process of assimilating people into our world it is common for them to be too affluent in our cultural Kinesics and leave the majority of their culture-specific kinesics. When we journey to the source of their cultures that we can see just the different ways that body language could appear! Take the example of kissing for instance. It is a common practice in the

Western world and throughout the other latitudes as well as longitudes, a kiss is two individuals putting their lips in a passionate, romantic style. If we are kissing in this manner it is displaying the kind of body language that provokes the most intense reaction from us. Certain groups of people who live in the arctic and subarctic regions of the globe Kissing is a totally different type of body language. It's that is a gesture of kissing the noses. Due to our kinesics culture that we have in the West such a kissing isn't likely to trigger the same emotion in our bodies... We might be able to find it awkward as well as funny! If you live in areas that are colder the kissing technique provokes the same reactions for them, just as kissing the lips would for those who live in the West. Take note of this especially traveling.

Connotation

One thing you should keep in mind regarding how the body language of a person can shift between cultures is that meanings change as well. Many thousands of years ago, when the language of our bodies was just beginning to find its feet across the globe, various groups from opposite sides of the globe were unable to discern the meaning of certain non-verbal signals in the context of each other's group. Due to this, it is not uncommon to find non-verbal clues which are still used in different civilizations today, which look identical, yet they mean something completely different. For instance, let's consider for instance the French for instance. In France the act of hugging is thought to be as a very intimate and touching act! According to the bodies language hierarchy there is a hierarchy of body language. The French manner of greeting one the other with bizarre (a kiss on both cheeks) is considered to be less intimate than hugging. In contrast, in nations like that of UK and Ireland hugging is less intimate in the chain of intimacy. To ensure that your relationships are secure between yourself and the people you meet from an ethnic background make sure you do an investigation into the fundamental body language of the cultural background. There is no requirement to speak fluently however it can be helpful!

In this section, we were taught about body language and how it is related to the two major genders, female and male. Additionally, we were introduced to different body language styles that are prevalent across the world. The main thing you should remember from this section is to research! If it's not completely planned, make sure not to go to an event with no knowledge of the criteria for culture expected by you to leave a lasting impression. If you're feeling overwhelmed, don't worry! Chapter 6 will provide you with some essential guidelines on how to behave your non-verbal self in a way that will help you succeed regardless of the situation or context!

Chapter 12: Body Language Tips

Since my last post up to now, I've been flooded you with details regarding body language, which includes its science-based basis and the motives behind it, and the possibilities of ways to interpret non-verbal signals. I've also provided the basics of how to control the overall tone of your body so that you can improve your coherence and conceal your feelings when they need to be. The time has come to take a deeper look at how you can control your body language to ensure that you will get the best possible results for you. These strategies will not only aid you in reaching the goals you set in all your interactions, but they'll additionally play an integral role to boost your self-esteem when you are in social interactions. Incorporating these suggestions to your day-to-day routines-- dealing with grocery shopping, or negotiating the latest deal with work, you can begin to notice positive outcomes over the course of your private life, which will show your self-esteem. your self! Achieving excellence in what we accomplish builds confidence which, in turn, results in a chain reaction of luck within our lives socially.

When it comes to confidence, it is impossible to get enough! If you're not engaged in a situation that has high-powered dynamics at stake It's a horrible feeling to know that you have the lack of confidence within your own self. If you're feeling depressed and unsure about the confidence level you should always take on a pose of power. How come super heroes do this every day? This is a great feeling! Certain poses for power include widening the stance of your body, having your palms downwards as well as reducing the distance between yourself and your companion.

Another method to build your confidence and self-esteem is to be aware of the voice of your self. The way you speak is to lower your voice when at the appropriate points during a conversation can give the impression of strength to the person whom you're interacting with. The lower frequencies resonate more deeply with the deeper parts of the population, which causes them to consider you in terms of a person, and perhaps, they will respect your character more. The reason for this is that high frequency frequencies tend to be connected to submissive or negative emotions like sadness (crying) as well as anxiety (shrieking and shouting). Maintaining a low voice and assertive helps you convey peace and calm with your non-verbal cues.

Are You Listening?

Additionally it is important to ensure that the person you're talking to feel that they're being acknowledged and heard. What would you think of your conversation partner did not seem to be listening and instead was concentrating more at intimidating you using a series of postures? Your self-confidence must not make other people drop theirs. Make them aware that you are concerned about what they're saying with your foot in front of the person, ensuring that you keep eye contact and nagging at points you're in agreement with. For spoken communication, people enjoy getting asked questions on the subject they're knowledgeable about. In the end, we are naturally self-centered. As a general rule, the most effective way to prove that you care about the message they're telling you is to demonstrate congruence as described in Chapter 4. You can mirror your conversation partner when you feel it is appropriate so that your subconscious feel that you're sharing the same thoughts.

Thanks, COVID.

Making sure you are on the same page of your subconscious that the other person is interfacing with by congruity can be a bit more difficult than pie, but it is possible. With COVID-19 as well as the increase in remote work opportunities for a lot of individuals, it's impossible to always be physically present with those we interact with. This is particularly true of interactions in work environments. A lot of organizations around the world due to COVID-19 have introduced a hybrid system of working at home and working in the office. This means that the use of online video conference has come to be the norm for a large number of employees. It has even extended to as interviewing candidates to fill positions within the company however this type of conversation is certainly among the most crucial one when it comes to the evaluation of the body language of a person! If you are someone who appreciates physical interaction, it ought to be the primary goal of your life to engage in the most interactions as you can in person. In addition, when conducting conversations or interviews, generally speaking it is best to get rid of any physical barriers that stand between you with the person you're talking to in order to get as much chance for a visual evaluation as possible.

Look at People's Feet for Added Insight

The removal of physical barriers between and your partner also provides you with an opportunity to analyze the non-verbal signals exhibited by feet that your person is interacting with. According to Phil Taylor, are, "the forgotten but most truthful area of nonverbal communication" (Taylor 2021). Examining a person's feet within the context of their movements can be the most enjoyable method of observing the overall tone of their body, especially when it comes to deep conversations or interviews. If you're looking for an additional perspective at the moment you interact with someone, look at the way their feet move (if they can be seen). If they're hidden in the dark, that person may be reluctant to discuss details, or not be comfortable with the topic. If they're tapping their feet or bouncing the feet around it could be that they are anxious or nervous. If the soles of their feet flat on the floor is the best indicator that the interaction is proceeding smoothly, particularly if your toes are pointed towards the ground.

Be the Real You!

When you keep all this in your mind, it's important to ensure that you don't completely lose your self in mastering the way you speak! Whatever an actor or actress you're your body is able to detect methods of recognizing the signs that something is not just right for a person. shifting your entire body language and swapping off all your normal body language for the spoken by someone that you aren't familiar with will surely create suspicion among those whom you come in contact with all the time (unless they've never even met previously; in which scenario, let them go crazy!). The main objective you should aim for in learning your body language skills is to keep those aspects of you that define you. They appreciate honesty and it will be evident that you build stronger, longer-lasting relationships by maintaining your integrity throughout every interaction. Keep it simple!

To Connect Instantly With Someone, Shake Hands

Like I said before, handshakes prior to and following an interaction (when you need to and, of course, do not shake your cashier's hands at the store--that's just odd) can help you with a thorough study of your partner's body expression. In this regard but, shaking hands can be crucial to them as well. Handshakes with someone in the first moments of a conversation can be crucial to making a connection instantly between two (or more) individuals. A physical gesture between and the other person, in conjunction with the force of your handshake, and the subconscious intentions it lays out for the other party is what can start the conversation. the conversation to start. Handshakes are also fundamental manners especially when it comes to business interactions. Handshakes after a meeting can aid in establishing (or eliminate) the assumptions you had been believing about the exchange. Perhaps, for instance, you believed that it went smoothly; you were armed with all the authority and secured the deal! But, when you exchange hands with your counterpart in the exit area, the handshake appears weak and uninterested. It could be that the meeting didn't take as smoothly as it appeared...

Showing Agreement

We have discussed before learning the technique of congruity with regards to the body language you use is one of the most important factors in learning the practice of body language generally. When we don't agree with a person, our body language can be dissociated from theirs since we are no longer a part of the person or that subject. As an example, two people sitting together at a dining table could have a disagreement about how delicious the lobster is, the other partner may decide to take their hands, slouch into their chair and then fold their arms. If they'd agreed about how good the lobster was and had a disagreement about the lobster's taste, they could have continued hand in hand! If you're trying to gain what you want from a conversation it is important not to create an argument of any kind even when you do not agree with what people are saying. Although I strongly advocate the importance of being honest with yourself but I would like to remind you that achieving what you want is often about being in the same boat as those we wish to aid us to achieve our objectives. This isn't to say that you need to join some sort of cult, use the psychedelic drug, or be obsessed with happiness to get rid of all your worries But I'm saying you need to fine tune the congruence that your behavior reflects and the people you wish to establish a mutually an enjoyable and positive relationship with.

The pool of tips you can apply in order to improve your body language is powerful and deep! In this article we have covered the most fundamental and crucial aspects of your body language which you can refine to provide you with the motivation you need in order to reach your objectives. The goals you are aiming for could include getting your dream job, acquiring an ideal employee, or securing the criminal within their internet of lies or enhancing your relationships with others by understanding and responding to those who surround you in a more effective manner. This article has presented you with the idea of being attentive during conversations, by showing you're attentive, and demonstrating your commitment to make the others feel appreciated and held to. In addition I highlighted the importance of having physical contact in an interaction for example, a hearty shake before and after the event for instant connections. In the final section, I discussed physical congruity as well as removing any obstacles between you and the person who is interacting with you in order to be able to read the body language of your friend in an comprehensive manner, and guarantee an easy connection between the two of you. Once that's done we can move onto the most common gestures and movements which we humans use daily, and the best way interpret them according to the context.

Chapter 13: Popular Gestures and Actions

For the first chapter of this one in a positive way, I'd like to emphasize something in the beginning: If you attempted to put all the most popular types of non-verbal languages from around the globe into a concise summary to study it would need been reincarnated numerous times in order to get the entire spectrum. This is why it's crucial to view your research into body language as a constantly evolving and evolving experience that doesn't actually have a definitive 'end in itself. This chapter is intended to utilize some of the most popular Western non-verbal cues for examples of what we would consider "popular" non-verbal cues within western cultural context, but the true lesson is the ability to recognize universal signals. The signals I will discuss in this chapter have been in existence for a long time while other cues (such like picking up imaginary particles of lint) were created as a result of the progress of mankind over time and with the development of modern items (such as clothing!). Since the advent of'mesmes', popular non-verbal cues are gaining traction in the charts of frequency, which indicates that individuals are expressing their feelings via non-verbal cues in conversations. Mini-cues that are non-verbal, like the 'whip' or "dab," are something worth studying to understand the way we humans relate with one another through social interaction so that we can express our sophisticated emotions.

Straddling a Chair

There are many movies where one of the characters at one point or the other, sits on an armchair so that their legs lie on either the other side or the rear of the chair is placed against their chests. Sometimes, they go an additional mile by folding their arms over the back of the chair while conversing. It's important to remember in this context that a significant portion of the body language that we use as a global society of today is the result of the primitive human beings who lived many thousands of years prior to us. In this regard with regard to sitting in a chair, research scientist J. Foster says it's worthwhile to think about defensive mechanisms that existed hundreds and possibly hundreds of years ago in the days when shields was in use during battle (Foster 2020c). Like shields, modern people are conditioned to shield the weakest areas of their bodies when they are in danger by someone they've met (because it's not like you would walk across a table in front of someone you don't know... do?). The back of the chair as a "shield" in a way allows the person to be in control of the conversation in an overwhelming manner because they are vulnerable and they aren't. You can regain some control by shifting yourself to the point that you're in front of the person, and there's no cushion to cover the back of their head.

Picking Imaginary Lint

The next item on Foster's list, which is a compilation of the most popular actions is making a fake lint splatter from clothes. If you're in the middle of an interaction it's important to make sure you check in to your partner each time you have a chance to check for an agreement. This is particularly important when you are trying to conclude a significant agreement at work, an environment where consensus is crucial to the success of your project. If someone is taking linty pieces from their clothes (especially even if the clothing appears to be in perfect good condition) This could indicate the person is either completely opposed with or want to express their opinions about something you've said (Foster 2020a). But, be cautious! Incorrectly interpreting that someone is opposing your views or taking lint off their clothes may result in a unintentional pause in your conversation. If you think you've made the right conclusion, but (for example, the person you are talking to picks up imaginary lint whenever you say an assertion) ensure that you take the effort to express their opinions. Foster states that when we lean back, and open our hands upwards in the event of inviting an interaction partner to express their opinions and ideas, we are able to resolve any disputes with respect and politeness. manner (Foster 2020a).

Head Gestures

The non-verbal signals which we emit through the movements of our heads are the most reliable for identifying the truth. For head movements that are popular, gestures, I'm certain you are aware that head nods as well as shaking the head are two of the most popular and well-known gestures around the world. If the rest of our body fails, we are able to use our heads to provide the most basic of answers to all questions such as "yes" or "no.'

As I explained in my previous post studying the motion of someone's head as they are talking to you will tell you something about the degree of their agreement with the words you are saying. Foster says that the very first gesture that humans are taught to use during their lifetime is the head shake or the word 'no' (Foster, 2020b). However it's extremely difficult to manage the natural motion in our heads if we do not agree with the subject matter. If you're uncertain about whether your contact likes you about a specific subject, you can ask them a "yes or no" query regarding that subject such as: "Are you sure you will have that report in on time?" If they don't nod or speak positively, watch closer for a slight shift of the head one side to the other. That could suggest that you require another employee to assist.

Basic Head Positions

While studying the most the most popular head movements we shouldn't be able to concentrate on understanding only agreements or disagreement. There are a myriad of other feelings that individuals can experience about us, and wish to communicate. Let's look at the top three head postures used in interactions as well as what they often mean.

One of the first positions that your interlocutor could display is one of neutrality. This means that the head of your friend could be in neutral positions that is level with your eyes with their heads at an angle of straightness (tilted either way) as well as the occasional acknowledgment that the information they're hearing from you is authentic. The head's position could indicate you're stuck in a conversational limbo. when you're attending a business gathering You might need increase your level of engagement in order to attract attention!

In terms of curiosity, Foster tells us that whenever people are struck by something fascinating in conversation they want to learn greater detail about, they are likely to turn their heads to the opposite side in order to provide a sort signal to the speaker to go on with the subject (Foster 2020). However when someone is making a judgment or internalizing a criticism of something that you've said to them and they are judging something, they might be inclined to tilt their head backwards as they are taking in their own internal thoughts. What you should do in this situation is to elicit either a head tilt or upward tilt of the chin to restore the trust of your audience.

Both Hands Behind Head

A final head-to-head gesture I'd like to make people aware of placing your hands over the head. According to Foster this specific gesture is usually performed by sales professionals business, along with lawyers and those who need to convince to earn an income (Foster 2020b). For putting it into an easy way for you to understand placing one's hands on their head is a demonstration of absolute confidence. The person who does this is assured to the top and to the point that they hold the upper hand on your conversation, whether via knowledge or effective conversational playing. The person may be making this technique to deter you or maybe they're just so excited by their own confidence and need the confidence to display it in some way! We'll look at how you can take on this powerful move in this moment as well as how to get your partner to return to more of a neutral posture.

If your friend whips their hands, and then folds the hands behind their heads and folds them behind their head, they're likely to sit back on their chairs as if being comfortable (because doing this standing up is a bit odd and is also a crime!). If you wish to appear as a person of equal standing and not be a threat, the best approach is to imitate their gesture precisely, however at a low level. If you're unimpressed with their attempts to be dominant but want to go back to the discussion in front of you, place an object that is out of grasp and start talking about the subject until they're required to sit up in the direction of this object. When they are forced back to neutral, you can carry on the conversation as you wish it to.

Seated Readiness

With COVID-19 and the growth of internet-based communication, it's now extremely difficult to determine the overall body language of the people we meet However, I've already discussed this before. This reason for me to mention this again is that analyzing the body language of a person when they sit can be vital when it comes down to closing sales and ending any interaction completely. When it comes to the concept of seated ready, it's crucial to be aware that it can only be applicable to situations in where we have an unobstructed image of a person's body while they are sitting directly in front of us. What is exactly seated readiness? Foster describes seated readiness for the audience in a manner which reminds me of a phrase you may remember. Have you ever watched a scary or thriller film, then remarked afterwards that you had been "on the edge of your seat"? Foster's explanation for the concept of seated readiness, he compares the amount that an individual sits forward to the degree of curiosity they show in the speaker in addition to the subject of discussion (Foster 2021). Also, if the person you are talking to is looking towards you when you talk, they're probably very interested about what you've got to discuss. But If they're slouching or leaning back or folding their arms they could not really care about the conversation in general (Foster 2021).

The Starter's Position

Concerning sitting readiness and the ability to lean forward and back into your chair, it's important to become familiar with the"starter's" position. This position is described as "sitting at the edge of the chair with one of the feet forward in a pose like a sprinter about to run out of the starting blocks" (profimpressions.com, 2014). In the section before the general consensus is that when someone is sitting forward when they interact that they're engaged and interested in the person and your interaction. As we realize, this isn't all the time.

In the beginning, I'd like to emphasize how crucial the context of every encounter you have regardless of how large or insignificant! Secondly, within the context of the position of the leader, if one leans forward in their chair this way (especially the moment they top it off with placing their hands in their knees) it is a sign that they plan for the end of their interaction whether you're prepared for it to come to an end or otherwise. However, it could suggest that the person you are talking to is tired, would prefer to go somewhere else or has had enough. In this case then it's the time to get your big guns out and present the most exciting aspect of your proposal to grab their attention and get straight to the point. This is because you and your partner might just being talking. If that's the case, and in the event that you've offended someone in any way, it's entirely dependent on the the context of why they are so quick to prefer to have the conversation ended.

Sexual Aggressiveness

On the last list of most frequently used non-verbal signals to learn about is sexual aggression. Before jumping into conclusion (another expression to keep in your pocket!) Sexual aggression in the in this article does not necessarily occur to you. Though aggressive body language used in sexual encounters is definitely one aspect to be studied but we'll be focusing on sexual aggression as it is perceived by people before a sexual exchange is initiated.

In the present, it's getting more and more commonplace for both men as well as women to employ the same types of non-verbal signals to express their sexuality. A very well-known expressions that we observe, both in the real world as well as on TV it is attaching the thumbs to the waistband or belt of a pair of jeans, and turning the hands down to indicate that you are framing others' attention towards our sexual organs (Foster 2022). The gesture, specifically it is designed to attract the attention of possible partners. If there is a desire for specific individuals it is possible to perform this action with the additional indication of moving their feet in the direction. Finally, Foster explains to us that when we're looking at someone particularly interested in sexually the pupils of our eyes tend to grow (Foster 2022). This type of language can be classified as aggressive, the current language tends to be more forward.'

For the final part, in this chapter, we have covered the most famous and well recognized non-verbal signals that you are familiar with as well as mostly, watch and use throughout the world. In the next chapter I will show you to apply the new skills of observation you've learned to good use, both in broad and specific contexts.

Chapter 14: Observing Subtle and Not-So-Subtle Cues

To date I've taken you through all the angles you have to consider in studying the body language of other people. It's time for you to put these abilities to use. It is a matter of what do you have to gain from being able to use all of these fantastic capabilities if you do not be able to know where to begin? In this section I'll show you to recognize indications that someone does not realize they are displaying non-verbal cues which don't align to their physical movements. The signals can be blatant all the time for those who are adept at hiding information from the world they could seem like finding the needle within a haystack. I'm sure you'll find it, but finding this needle is definitely more than worth the effort!

Body Language as Non-Verbal Communication

For the first chapter of this one in a positive way, I'd like make it clear that in the event that you were to assume that body language (i.e. non-verbal signals) weren't present humans by itself could be extremely boring. Do you think of every interaction you have only of you sitting in a stoic, unmoving posture as you communicate verbally with your partner in conversation? There are many situations that we are unable to speak to each other also that's why communication using our bodies is crucial. We should take the time to consider the value of our body, from toe to head, and the places we'd be without them to assist us in getting our message through.

Body Language From Head to Toe

Beginning at the top If we didn't have head we'd not even exist! The heads of our bodies (our faces along with our shoulders and necks) are the first thing we stare at and talk to. Our brains are held by them which means that we'd be ineffective without them.

Our midsections (our arm and torsos) are essential for communicating via non-verbal signals like breath, waving, shaking hands, and much more. If our torsos were not there (we could, in fact, have died, but let's not get caught up in that) and arms, we would be unable to be able to communicate verbally or have significant physical contact with our friends and acquaintances.

The bottom of our bodies (from the waist downwards) could be among the most significant part of us, when we are trying to discern subtle non-verbal clues.

Without our bottoms being unable to express ourselves in our most authentic way; i.e., our unconscious mind wouldn't have access to.

When you take into consideration the three different parts of our body from head up to the toes, you'll be able to bet on the importance to pay attention to the complete bodies of people whom you meet. This is because watching and analysing only one element of the body an time will not be enough for you to make a precise decision about what that you're seeking. The human body doesn't perform one movement at a given time. They use a variety of gestures rapidly in quick succession and at very high frequency throughout their interactions, based on the message they're trying to convey. Understanding how to recognize patterns of gestures, and then learning to link them the other ones in your brain, is crucial to forming your own theories and conclusions in the highest degree of accuracy.

How the Arms Convey Meaning

Take a moment to concentrate on our midsections of our bodies and, specifically, our hands and arms. It's not difficult to realize that a large portion of the way we convey our thoughts and communicate messages during our interactions happens with our hands and arms! Let's take a look at the hands first and then consider how they could be used to communicate in our everyday lives.

Consider, for instance on schools. It can be painful to think of the time when you were plagued by anxiety, and you was not yet something that was coherent and aware. When we look at the cultural messages that are associated with schools there are numerous examples! Examples include the raising of one's arm in order to draw the attention of the teacher so it is possible to ask (or respond to) an inquiry.

Along with our hands, and our arms can do as well (if not as much) in expressing our personalities in interactions. And there are endless examples. Hands point to objects, wave to people, punch individuals and objects, turn each to the side, make the peace symbol, put hands in prayer, as and also to make images like the heart of love--and many more! Our hands are incredibly essential in transmitting meaning since they can accomplish so many things, make so many different symbols and signs. But, the most important thing is that they convey the things that words are unable to. Consider deaf individuals and their sign language, as an example. The evolution of our brains has given us with a universal language made of non-verbal signals that are executed with the hands! This is just how intricate and complex these areas of our body are.

Handshakes

To put this into perspective I've previously talked about the significance of handshakes when it comes to conversations with people. Although handshakes are fantastic in establishing a direct bond with others at the very beginning of a interaction as well as for sharing feelings prior to and after interactions, they're additionally extremely effective for communicating specific emotions in situations where words don't suffice. For instance funerals. If someone dear to mine is deceased and we're gathered in my home following the funeral, you may approach me, perhaps as a friend from the workplace who isn't familiar with me sufficient to wrap me in a huge hug. Instead, you choose an exchange of hands that lasts for just a few seconds more than the norm and is accompanied by an eye contact that, without words, shows me how sympathetic you feel about my current situation.

Using the Hand to Touch the Other Negotiator

In addition it is possible to use your hands free during your handshake. You can reach out and grab me by my bicipital, giving me a strong grip of assurance. Touch increases our connection and allows us to bond with a greater emotional connection by using our non-verbal signals. To express my gratitude for your compassion and kindness gesture, and since I'm not dissatisfied about the way you choose to show me comfort and show my the same body language as you do in imitation of your gesture, by gripping my Bicep using my hands.

Hand on the Shoulder

As we're discussing the subject of touching our hands with others, a popular location to hold your hands in a meaningful manner during interactions is on the shoulders. Like gripping the part of the bicep that is used during a genuine handshake, gripping your shoulder (while shaking hands, or otherwise) is also seen as an act of affection as well as comfort, empathy, or sympathy. There is a very low chance that you will see someone gripping your shoulder to show strength or authority in the absence of clapping the hands of your shoulders as a result. That is, you are grabbing your shoulders with force, but only within a particular context. In the majority of cases but, the positioning of a hand onto one's shoulder is not an aggressive gesture, and shouldn't be considered as such.

Hand on the Elbow

Similar to placing your arm on the elbow of someone in a conversation isn't usually thought of as a hostile gesture. One of the most frequent instances in the time a person puts their fingers on, or grasps another's elbow, is during an exchange of hands. The reason for this is that the elbow's bent and is easily reachable by the person in front of it. In addition, the grasping of elbows that are opposite in the handshaking procedure occurs most frequently in formal, business-related interactions in which the two parties are not in a casual or friendly connection with one another.

This means that the interaction between them is solely upon their professional obligations.

Legs and Posture

When it comes to cues that might not be as clear as we believe that they are, consider the posture of your legs as well as general posture of those who you are in contact with. In some instances, the posture of a person can be easily read (for instance, a teen who is slouching, and appears to be disinterested implies that they are) However, a lot often it will be difficult to determine what a person's posture individual means. While you're observing the leg posture and posture of your friend take note of their shoulders as well as the angle of their legs (keep your mind that this scenario is applicable to those who are sitting). If they have straight shoulders that means they feel neutral regarding the current situation. However, the shoulders that are angled back or forward could indicate that they are engaged or not interested in the discussion. It is the same regarding where their knees are pointed!

Ankles and Feet

As you go down your body, how a person moves their feet when they interact will tell you something about the way they feel. One of the most evident signals to look out for is the way your ankles are positioned which are crossed or not. An ankle that is not crossed means your participant feels, if not in a tangible way that they are comfortable with both you and your interaction in general. However the ankles that are crossed could indicate that they're feeling restricted and unwilling to speak. Like ankles, how the direction their feet are pointed (as I've discussed in earlier chapters) could reveal much about how they really feel about the person they are talking to and overall.

Hugs

In the next section, we will discuss an intimate and personal body language Let's discuss hugging! The act of hugging is one of the most normal human interactions which can occur between two individuals. Hugs are a sign of being feeling happy, joyful or sad, mourning or maybe angry and even hurt. Furthermore, the hugs we share can carry various degrees of intimacy associated with their recipients, based on the individual we're the person we are hugging. It's likely that we're all acquainted with that awkward hug in which we hug, but don't actually mold our bodies according to the person we are hugging. If you look at that kind of hug to the way we embrace our spouse or parents, the differences in the intimacy of hugs becomes apparent. Knowing how to determine the amount of affection someone hugs you is a fantastic method to gauge how connected you feel as a human being in the sense of relationship and comfort.

Concealment of Body Language

In terms of hiding the emotions we feel and our raw emotions via our body language those signals can be difficult to detect as you might think. The reason behind this is because we are social beings and the growth of our societies around the world has created an (toxic when you ask me) society where people are required to display a positive friendly, outgoing, and open appearance every single moment. Because of this, our personalities have changed to reflect the authentic self, as well as those we display to others. In this regard next time you're debating a tough subject with someone who you think may not be willing to discuss the truth take note of the amount or extent to which the person is communicating non-verbally relation to their verbal expressions. It will show a huge distinction in their ratio.

Low-Energy Body Language

In the case of example, you believe that the person with whom that you're talking to is uninterested with the subject in question, or they are being questioned about certain information that you think they're not willing to discuss the amount of time they speak to each other may begin to rise. This could be a strategy by them to divert attention from the discomfort they are experiencing by doing something like making it appear as though they're comfortable talking about the subject. As you notice that your conversation is getting highly verbal It is the time to be aware of the signs that are not verbal. It could be that your conversation partner has lost their voice This is due to the fact that they're focusing all their attention on swiping through the data they do not want to divulge.

Controlling Hand Gestures

Before you leap to conclusions and think that I'm about to teach the art of dominating the people around you with your hands this article is focused on learning to be able to detect those who you are in contact with are conscious of their hands. Though many of the hand movements we employ in our daily interactions are natural to us, some interactions (particularly ones where you are playing with the hand that is upper) could cause someone to notice their actions and how they are expressing themselves. Be aware of how the person you are talking to uses their hands when they are talking If they suddenly alter their behavior and display unusual hand movements in comparison to the gestures they used prior to that, they may be aware that the way they express themselves is important!

Exaggerated Body Language

If someone is conscious the body language they use while in the course of a conversation, this increased awareness could hinder their ability to manage how they interact to us, even if it's not verbally. It's true that it's not like we're all as actors or actresses. And certain of us will never master the art of putting on an act without appearing unreal. If you're not having a conversation with someone else who is acting professionally and knows as much about body communication as you are so it shouldn't be difficult to recognize those who attempt to be a bit difficult. The reason for this is that movements that are usually perceived as subtle get over-exaggerated in order to get you to notice them and consider what the person is trying to get you thinking. They're trying to get your attention the gesture that they believe can cause you to react to a specific way, but what they're doing is revealing to you how they're acting in order to alter the tone of conversation. after you have figured this out it is possible to shift the control back to yourself!

When you have all these subtle as well as not so subtle signals in your mind I'm sure you've discovered the real lesson of this section: If you are as knowledgeable about body communication as you do today it is impossible to find a things as subtle signals! With your knowledge and experience, that you're preparing your body to recognize various cues throughout all of your body. after you've picked to them you can simply go back to understanding the context in order to find the right answers. In the next section we will look at a topic that is fun, but one that shouldn't be thought of in the study of the body communication.